P9-CCQ-697

The Panasonic Way

The Panasonic Way

Toshihiko Yamashita

From a Chief Executive's Desk

Translated by Frank Baldwin

KODANSHA INTERNATIONAL
Tokyo and New York

First published in Japanese in 1987 by Toyo Keizai Shinposha under the title of *Boku demo shacho ga tsutomatta.*

Distributed in the United States by Kodansha International/ USA Ltd., 114 Fifth Avenue, New York, New York 10011.

Published by Kodansha International Ltd., 2-2 Otowa 1-chome, Bunkyo-ku, Tokyo 112 and Kodansha International/ USA Ltd., 114 Fifth Avenue, New York, New York 10011. Copyright © 1987 by Toshihiko Yamashita. English translation copyright © 1989 by Kodansha International Ltd. All rights reserved. Printed in Japan.

First edition, 1989

Library of Congress Cataloging-in-Publication Data

Yamashita, Toshihiko, 1919–
   The Panasonic way.

   Translation of: Boku de mo shachō ga tsutomatta.
   1. Yamashita, Toshihiko, 1919–   . 2. Industrialists—Japan—Biography. 3. Electric Industries—Japan—History. 4. Matsushita Denki Sangyō—Biography.
5. Electronic industries—History. I. Title.
HD9697.A2Y3513 1988   338.7′621381′0924 [B]   88-80133
ISBN 0-87011-890-0 (U.S.)
ISBN 4-7700-1390-6 (Japan)

CONTENTS

Prologue

I shall never forget Saturday, January 8, 1977. The private secretary to Konosuke Matsushita, founder of Matsushita Electric Industrial Co.,Ltd. and executive advisor since 1973, called me at home and said Mr. Matsushita wanted to see me on Monday morning. He didn't say what it was about, and I felt I couldn't ask. I agreed to be there at ten o'clock.

The next evening I was having some saké as a nightcap when the phone rang. It was Hirozo Tanimura, one of the four executive vice presidents of Matsushita Electric and a former boss of mine.

"Did you get a call from Mr. Matsushita?"

"Yes, yesterday. I am to see him tomorrow."

"He may have a tough proposition for you, but don't say no right then and there. It's a very serious matter."

Of course, I realized something important was in the wind, but I had no idea what. I was nervous when I arrived at Mr. Matsushita's office on Monday morning. He didn't mince words.

"Board Chairman Arataro Takahashi is resigning and my son-in-law, Masaharu, will take over his duties. I want you to become president."

I was speechless. For an instant I wondered if Mr. Matsushita was becoming senile. I had been named to the board of directors only three years earlier. Of the twenty-six directors who attended board meetings, I was the second most junior. Completely immersed in my job as head of the air conditioner division, I had never even thought about running the whole corporation!

"I must respectfully decline. I could not handle the job," I said.

"This is a bit of a shock, I know, and I don't expect you to give me an answer right now. Think it over carefully," he said.

I left his office in a daze. There was the Annual Management Policy Meeting that afternoon and a party afterwards. Several vice presidents and the director in charge of personnel asked me, "What happened at your meeting with Mr. Matsushita?" Everybody seemed to know about the summons. Better turn down the offer quickly before the situation gets out of hand, I thought. Two days later Mr. Matsushita called me in and asked what I had decided.

"Were you serious about what you said?" I replied. "I could not possibly accept the position."

"Don't say that. Consider it some more."

At home that evening I was pondering my dilemma over a cup of saké, when Masaharu Matsushita called me.

"I understand you refused, but I hope you'll change your mind," he said.

"I've been drinking. I'll call you tomorrow," I said and hung up. Tension had made me short-tempered. He was the founder's son, after all.

The next day I went to the senior Matsushita's office determined to turn down the job.

"Did you think it over?"

"Yes, sir. I cannot accept the presidency."

"Okay. If that's your answer, I won't try to pressure you. It's unfortunate for the company, but that's too bad. I want you to know that I was completely serious. Offering the position to you is not something I'd do lightly. Don't forget that."

I thought the matter was closed, but Mr. Matsushita had just begun his strategy. On the way back to my division, his son Masaharu stopped me in the hall and invited me into his office. He said this was a crucial period for the company and urged me to take the top spot. Later the telephone calls started. Colleagues and others said it was my duty to accept and promised their cooperation. I began to feel trapped, as if I were being disloyal in rejecting the offer. I conferred with Seiji Miyoshi, a former boss of mine who was then president of a subsidiary, Matsushita Electronics Corporation.

"Are you going to take the position?" he asked.

"It looks like I'll have to. I don't have any choice."

"If you become president, are you going to order me around? If you do, I won't listen to you."

That drove home to me the problem of my junior status. I should decline, I thought. Shortly afterwards, the president of the Matsushita union made an appointment to see me. Even union officials knew about my selection! Now I was desperate. I couldn't let it appear as if the union had persuaded me to accept the position. The time for vacillation was over: I decided to become the third president of Matsushita Electric.

When I told Mr. Matsushita, he said, "If you have any conditions about taking the position, let me know them now." I didn't have any. Reluctant as I was to become president, I brought no private agenda to the post.

I still remember how unpleasant the whole business was. If I had sought the post, it would have been a time of triumph. Instead, I felt like some kind of freak on display. Everybody had some opinion about me: "He's too young!" " Why him?" "He'll never make it." Many were far from convinced that I was the right man for the job, and I was not the consensus choice. The press dubbed my promotion over my many superiors the "Yamashita leap," after the famous jump by gymnast Hiro Yamashita that won him a gold medal at the 1964 Tokyo Olympics. The difference was that I was an unenthusiastic contender. At the press conference to announce my appointment, I said, "Those who selected me also bear considerable responsibility." Although it may have sounded like conventional self-deprecation, that was how I really felt. Fortunately, newly appointed Board Chairman Masaharu Matsushita supported me at every step of the way.

One day in July 1977, after I had been on the job about five months, the elder Matsushita dropped by my office. He was smiling so I figured he had not come to chew me out.

"How are things going?"

"I'm surviving."

"Good. Here, take this." He handed me an envelope.

"What is it?"

"A little pocket money. I've already paid the tax on it so use it any way you want."

"It is very kind of you but . . ."

"Think nothing of it."

My salary at the time was only slightly higher than before, yet the presidency entailed formidable social obligations, especially giving gifts on such occasions as the marriage of subordinates, or when their children graduated from college. It was typical of Mr. Matsushita to sympathize with my plight: the envelope contained ¥1 million (about $4,000 then), and it came in very handy. I received another "emergency bonus" at the end of the year. From 1978 my salary and bonus were raised, and I could manage on my own.

Having accepted the presidency, it would have been dishonorable to quit, no matter what happened. I saw myself as a relief pitcher who would finish at least one two-year stint. Then I was asked to stay on for another term "to continue what you have started," and I agreed. A good relief hurler can throw hard for about four innings. Mr. Matsushita had asked me to stay on for "a decade," but I wanted to step down earlier. As it turned out, I pitched a nine-inning game, from 1977 to 1986.

1
Early Days

I was born in July 1919 in the heart of Osaka, the Nishinoda section, the first of three sons. My father died during my senior year in high school. Because of his poor health, I knew early on that I would have to help support the family. That was one reason why I had chosen Osaka Municipal Izuo Technical High School, which specialized in the sciences. The training there was equivalent to that in a technical college today. Japan was industrializing rapidly, and competition for admission was stiff. I was a conscientious student, majored in glass-making and ceramics, and made average grades. No special honors or exploits distinguished me from my classmates. The famous coup attempt by radical young army officers on February 26, 1936, occurred in my junior year. At this period the military was growing more powerful at home and was preparing to expand across China. Nevertheless, I have happy memories of my teen-age years.

In 1986, when Izuo Technical High School celebrated its sixty-fifth anniversary, I was invited to speak there. It was the first time I had been back. The school was in the same place, but the wooden workshop building had been replaced by a modern ferroconcrete structure.

My father was a fairly sophisticated man for the times. He worked for a shipping company, traveled abroad on business, and spoke English. I don't remember much about him, but he seemed to enjoy the good things in life. It must have been very difficult for my mother after he died. I knew she had to make a lot of sacrifices for us, and I can still see her tired smile as she greeted me and my brothers after school and fixed us a snack.

Today Japan is affluent, and two children per family is the norm. The days of poor households struggling to feed and clothe ten kids or so are over, and children no longer learn values—frugality, the work ethic—from seeing their parents cope with adversity.

Prosperity is preferable to poverty, of course. But in the old days, the father was the head of the household, the breadwinner, and his word was law. Nowadays, he is taken for granted. That loss of authority has caused a rise in delinquency. The younger generation doesn't automatically defer to mom and dad. Parenting is much harder in the 1980s.

To digress briefly, the People's Republic of China, in an effort to control its burgeoning population, has restricted couples to only one child. Consequently, Chinese parents now give that kid expensive, fancy toys, much to the delight of Japanese toy makers, who are selling more than ever to China.

Upon graduation in 1937, I went to work for Matsushita Electric, then a medium-sized company with about 4,000 employees. I never dreamed it would become an industrial empire. My first assignment was a dull factory job. The work was monotonous and I was utterly bored. There were many little frustrations, and I often thought, "Is this what I want to do with my life?"

Then I happened to read Maksim Gorky's *The Lower Depths*. A statement by Sachin, the social outcast, hit me like a thunderbolt: "If you enjoy work, life is paradise. If work is a duty, life is hell." It was a home truth that I've never forgotten.

Attitude is everything. There is a profound difference between doing a task because you have to and doing it because you want to. Whether a job is boring or fascinating is in the mind of the worker. Later, in Confucius's *Analects*, I read, " To prefer the Way is better than only to know it. To delight in the Way is better than merely to prefer it." Enjoying a job enables you to do it well; outlook is crucial. These two bits of wisdom from a Russian novelist and a Chinese philosopher shaped my approach to life.

The fighting in China expanded into the Pacific War in December 1941, and many of my friends were drafted. I was classified as an engineer and exempted from military service. In March 1944, I married Kikuko. We were cousins and knew each other's temperament well, and relatives and friends were enthusiastic about our marriage, saying we were well suited. Because it was wartime, we had a simple wedding followed by a small reception for relatives at our house.

My life took a dramatic turn after Japan's surrender on August 15, 1945. General Douglas MacArthur, the Supreme Commander for the Allied Powers (SCAP), initiated sweeping reforms of Japanese society, including so-called economic democratization. The great industrial and financial conglomerates—*zaibatsu*—that had dominated Japan's economy were broken up. In March 1946, SCAP mistakenly classified Matsushita Electric as a *zaibatsu* and ordered the company dissolved. Actually we were a small outfit compared to giants like Mitsui, Mitsubishi, Yasuda, and Sumitomo, and SCAP later realized its error. In any event, Matsushita's electric light bulb factory became an independent company run by Hirozo Tanimura, who was then my boss, and I went with him. Later, when the company did poorly, he returned to Matsushita and I moved to a different light bulb maker. In 1952, Tanimura asked me to join a new joint venture Matsushita was forming, saying they were short of engineers my age.

Having once resigned from Matsushita, I was reluctant to return. Tanimura saw this and gave me some advice: "Matsushita doesn't need you. There are plenty of people here with your background. But this is a much bigger operation than your present one. You'll have a chance to show your ability. I asked you to come back for your sake, not Matsushita's." There seemed no point in letting pride stand in the way of opportunity. This was a major turning point in my life. A strange karma seemed to link Tanimura and me, and I was fortunate to know this kind, frank man.

Learning from Philips

In 1951, Konosuke Matsushita toured the United States and Europe. Impressed by America's wealth and power, he decided Matsushita Electric should link up with a foreign electronics maker and chose N. V. Philips' Gloeilampenfabrieken of the Netherlands. After tough negotiations a joint venture was formed—Matsushita Electronics Corporation—and I joined it in 1954. Under the agreement, Philips provided the technology and Matsushita the management know-how. Seiji Miyoshi was the senior Japanese executive and he later became chairman of the board. A temperamental man with a strong personality, Miyoshi was much feared by his subordinates. Actually, many of the senior Matsushita executives then were tough cookies, but Miyoshi was the toughest. He drove people hard and wouldn't take no for an answer.

One day he made a particularly outrageous demand. I thought it was wrong and made my objections clear.

"I don't need an incompetent guy like you around. Get lost!" he said.

"Goodbye," I said, and I went home.

That night I heard my wife talking to someone at the front door. I went out to see who it was and found Miyoshi there. "I happened to be in the area and decided to drop in," he said. Of course, he didn't "happen" by; it was his crusty way of restoring peace.

In both 1958 and 1961, I spent several months studying new technology at Philips headquarters in Eindhoven, a rural town about an hour from Amsterdam. I was put up in a hotel, more like a boarding house actually, where Philips housed all its visitors. Except for the beautiful landscape, it was unimpressive by Japanese standards. My room was sparsely furnished and the food was simple. A fellow guest, a government official from a Middle Eastern country, constantly complained about the plainness of the accommodations. Philips executives stayed there with their families, so it wasn't that bad. Philips employees often invited me to their homes, and I noticed that they all lived rather frugally. Although Japan was still a poor country in the late 1950s, by comparison the Japanese ate luxuriously.

Plant visitors had lunch in the guest dining room. There was always a small Japanese flag at my seat, a touching gesture. When I heard the waitresses asking one another, "What country's flag is that?" I told them, "Japan. It's in Asia." They had no idea of Far Eastern geography. I asked for a world map but found to my chagrin that Holland was in the middle and Japan wasn't on it at all! Pointing to the right of the Asian mainland, I said, "Japan is located about here." "I thought that was China," a waitress said. I remember thinking, "Cartography is a very subjective science."

Part of my training was at a factory that produced vacuum tubes and electric light bulbs. The plant had the latest equipment, and the technology was far ahead of Matsushita's. Job and status distinctions were designated by the colors of uniforms: dark blue for ordinary workers, light gray for foremen, and white overalls for supervisors. Section chiefs and above wore suits. The lighter the color, the less likely that the person was involved in dirty work. "The advanced industrialized countries sure do things differently from Japan," I thought.

Philips had rigorous cost controls. When the sales department requested an escort for visitors, for example, the factory calculated the costs according to the guide's position: so much for a section chief, more for a director. It was a cost-conscious, rational system. By comparison, Matsushita was very casual. Escorts were arranged through personal contacts. They were a favor, part of the web of human relationships that supports Japanese-style management.

Philips had a systematic, logical organizational setup. If a department head was an engineer, his assistant had a liberal arts background. The next supervisor down the chain of command was technically trained, and so on. Department chiefs, not the personnel office, picked their own successors. The ability to make that kind of decision was considered an essential managerial skill.

Weekends in Holland were great fun. Each Saturday a different division chief invited me to his home for dinner. The hospitality was wonderful, and I was made to feel like part of the family. On Sundays, I was often taken to local places of interest. The Dutch are wonderful hosts, and their European heritage has accustomed them to meeting people from different cultures.

A Hard Time at West Electric

In 1962, Matsushita Electric named me managing director of West Electric, a Matsushita Electronics Corporation affiliate that made strobes. My instructions were to help straighten out the technological problems but not to get involved in management. The owner was a hard-nosed entrepreneur who ran things his way. West's problems were supposedly due to outdated equipment. Improve the quality and it will start making a profit again, I was told. Little did I know.

On the first day I was embroiled in nasty labor negotiations. West was losing money, wages were low, and the union was militant. The union leader had been forced out of Matsushita Electric during the 1950 purge of Communists and left-wingers in the public and private sectors. Hostile to West's owner, he frequently called short work stoppages. Without better labor–

management relations, the situation was hopeless. The owner, a sharp businessman, had managed to conceal his labor problems.

The union chief seemed conciliatory. "I'm glad you are here, Yamashita-san," he used to say, but his methods were coercive and uncompromising. We needed money to settle the wage demands. Hat in hand, I went to Matsushita Electric for help. The response was, "You were assigned to West from Matsushita Electronics Corporation. Get the funds from them." Rebuffed, I took my begging bowl there. Their line was, "You left here and went back to the main company, which then transferred you to West. Get the money from the head office." I felt as if I did not belong to any company as each, as it were, passed the buck but not the bucks. Furious and at a loss where to turn, I finally asked Kuninori Azuma, then with Matsushita Electric's battery division and later executive vice president of the company, and he arranged a loan. West employees got their raise, and production picked up.

But the labor troubles didn't stop. Every time an issue arose—wage negotiations, bonus demands, work rules—the union went on strike. The constant harassment included anti-management handbills stuck on the fence around my home, an outrageous embarrassment to me.

One evening the firebrand union leader showed up at my house. I invited him in, hoping we could have a serious man-to-man discussion over a few cups of saké. As the wine flowed, he got a little drunk and started making wild charges against Mr. Matsushita, the West owner, and all "capitalist bosses." The diatribe continued until he left. As luck would have it, a union member visiting a friend nearby saw him stagger out of my house, and the story quickly spread that the union leader had gotten drunk at a company executive's home. It destroyed his credibility with the rank and file, who thereafter ignored his calls for radical action. Negotiations with the union became much easier and we soon had the situation under control.

Having posters calling you an exploiting swine pasted on your house is not a pleasant experience, but I didn't let it bother me. The teen-age girl who put up the handbills was a recent junior high school graduate who didn't understand the issues. She was just following union orders, and I felt sorry for her. After my erstwhile nemesis fell from grace, the union stopped such personal attacks.

When the strike was over and emotions had cooled, I called a joint meeting of union officials and company executives and had the accountant explain West's situation. The company was capitalized at ¥60 million, and its debts totaled ¥500 million. There wasn't enough cash on hand to meet the next payroll. I told the accountant neither to withhold bad news nor exaggerate our plight. He was to answer all questions except "How did the company get in this mess?" and "Who is responsible?" After he finished, I explained what management wanted to do and our plan for recovery.

The meeting lasted from morning until late at night. By the time we broke up, everybody understood the crisis. That was the first step in turning the company around. When a situation is crystal clear, usually the solution is obvious. Within two years the outlook had improved, and a year later we turned a profit.

My experience at West convinced me that "open management" works and it became an article of faith with me. When everybody pulls their weight in a small outfit like West, the results are quick and dramatic. There is a virtuous circle: improvement boosts morale, which generates even greater effort. I continued periodic "state of the company" reports to West employees.

I stayed at West Electric three years, of which only the first was rough. Toward the end I wasn't sure I wanted to go back to Matsushita.

My Cold War: The Air Conditioner Division

In 1965, I was put in charge of Matsushita's cooler (now air conditioner) division, the company's black sheep, with low market share, poor products, and weak sales channels. Matsushita had made its mark in consumer electric appliances, but its record with big machinery was spotty and unpromising. This was driven home to me shortly after I took over, when a consumer magazine, *Kurashi no techo*, brought out a special issue devoted to air conditioners. All the major brands were compared and Matsushita ranked lowest. I thought, "If our products are this bad, we deserve to be at the bottom." The next day I went to see the editor. I understood the magazine's obligation to its readers to report the results of product tests, I said, but Matsushita Electric is going to improve its air conditioners. If we succeeded, I hoped he would publish another rating.

I returned to my office and called a staff meeting. We brainstormed the problems, and I indicated what had to be done. "Until we are confident our new line of products is as good as those of our competitors, we won't put them on the market," I said. The disgrace of being "worst in the industry" was a powerful incentive. Thanks to excellent teamwork, our air conditioners improved dramatically.

I held the line on prices despite high production costs and an increase in the commodity tax. My superiors blanched at this policy, but I was convinced that if we could ride out the cost–price crunch, the division would be in a good competitive position. By 1969, we had the top market share in the industry.

Air conditioners are a seasonal product. Sales soar during a hot summer, but the stock piles up in warehouses if July and August are cold. The staff was fatalistic: "The weather is unpredictable," or "Ups and downs are the nature of the business." It seemed to me that everybody talked about the weather, but nobody did anything about it. When sales were good, the salesmen took the credit; when sales slumped, they blamed the temperature.

A natural phenomenon was a convenient scapegoat. Of course, we couldn't manipulate Mother Nature to sell cooling equipment, but we could at least devise different marketing strategies for hot and cool summers. I looked into how other businesses contended with the weather's vagaries and discovered we were not the only ones in this fix.

A Tokyo caterer, for example, supplied box lunches to Korakuen Stadium, home of the Yomiuri Giants, Japan's most popular professional baseball team. Night games usually start at six-thirty, and stadium vendors placed their order at about three, yet the caterer had to start making the lunches by eleven in the morning at the latest. If the game was rained out, he had to throw away three thousand lunches, a terrible loss for a small businessman. He couldn't sue the Weather Bureau for inaccurate forecasts: weathermen are immune to malpractice suits.

Frustrated, desperate even, the caterer discovered a rule-of-thumb forecasting method. On game days he went to the grandstand at Korakuen and looked across the city at the 1,003-foot-high Tokyo Tower. If the top was clearly visible, chances were it would not rain that night. If the top was obscured, even on fair days it rained in the evening. Amazingly, his unscientific technique proved a hundred percent accurate. This entrepreneur found a way to cope with the weather. Zeal will overcome most adversity.

Let me cite another example familiar to visitors to Ise Shrine, the sacred Shinto site in central Japan. The local delicacy there is a rice cake with red beans, or *akafukumochi*, which is prepared daily for the tourists and pilgrims who flock to the shrine. The number of visitors fluctuates enormously depending on the weather in nearby prefectures. For many years local merchants were at the mercy of cumulus clouds and low pressure zones. Underestimation meant lost sales and overproduction resulted in waste and financial loss until they found a way to predict attendance accurately. They checked ticket sales at major stations of private railways serving Ise and adjusted output accordingly.

Again, the key factor was determination. These merchants didn't shrug and say, "There's nothing we can do about the weather." That's defeatism. In business, you have to be single-minded and find answers to apparently insoluble problems. No one else will look after your interests. Resourcefulness is the corollary of determination.

Unlike box lunches and rice cakes, air conditioner sales do not vary sharply from day to day. However, there is a significant yearly fluctuation depending on summer temperatures. To find the basic rhythm, we first checked July temperatures in Osaka for the preceding twenty years, for forty percent of our annual sales were made in July. We discovered a close correlation between sales figures and days when the temperature exceeded 86° Fahrenheit (30° Celsius). Research showed that July 1954 was the coolest month, with only ten days with high temperatures. Top honors went to July 1973 with thirty scorchers. The average was twenty-one days.

Now we had solid data to work with. In planning production, we took into account that there were between ten and twenty-one days of unbearable heat in July. With this frame of reference, we scheduled year-round output. In early July, we checked the temperature pattern so far, sales figures to date, and forecasts, and, if necessary, increased production. Accurate planning reduced costs in every phase of the operation.

Proper planning is the bedrock of an enterprise. The planning stage is the time to get employee input—ideas and know-how—and examine every facet of the task. With a good plan, a project is sixty percent accomplished, partly because striving to meet the goals of a solid plan sparks enormous enthusiasm. Conversely, if production and sales targets are missed, you probably started with guesswork.

The seasonal character of the air conditioning industry allowed me time to think about planning. Later, as president, I became a real bear on the subject. As the Germans say, "The devil is in the details," and I was a stickler for careful analysis and projections.

For the skeptics, let me give a concrete example of goal-induced enthusiasm. New employees, including recent college graduates, join Matsushita each April and are assigned to the manufacturing divisions or sales for practical training. Demand for air conditioners picks up when the rainy season ends, about July 10. To be prepared, we raise production to a peak the first week in May, which by coincidence is Golden Week, so-called because of the several national holidays thereabouts: the Emperor's Birthday (April 29), Constitution Day (May 3), and Children's Day (May 5). From 1986, May 4 also became a national holiday, while organized labor has long celebrated May 1. Millions of people travel during that week, the second most popular holiday after New Year's, and the whole country is in a relaxed, festive mood. Nevertheless, the air conditioner division had a relatively ambitious plan one year, and everyone had pitched in to increase output. I enlisted—perhaps mobilized would be more accurate—the trainees for this effort.

I set up an assembly line with the new men and put them on the same no-time-off schedule as the rest of the division. At first they were not too happy. By Golden Week they had not had a single day off—no weekends, no national holidays— since joining the company five weeks earlier. It wasn't exactly the exciting business career they had anticipated. But gradually the neophytes realized they were responsible for that line and worked their butts off. When they met the production quota, the sacrifices made the triumph especially sweet.

In 1971, Matsushita Electric decided to build an air conditioner plant in Malaysia, the division's first overseas facility, in response to the Malaysian government's request for one. At the time, export demand was only about 20,000 units per year, which our factories in Japan could easily handle, but, with an eye to the future, a 100,000-unit plant was designed.

Some people in the air conditioner division opposed the idea on the grounds that it was both too expensive and premature. Division figures showed the plant would not come close to breaking even. Nevertheless, it was important for Matsushita to accommodate the Malaysian government.

Earlier offshore facilities had been built to supply only the host country, and they were relatively small-scale operations that produced a variety of products. The Malaysian venture, however, was an export-oriented factory, and the quality had to be as good as in Japan. Instead of the usual assembly operation, all air conditioner parts—compressors, motors, and so on—were to be made there.

I visited the facility about a dozen times, and frankly I had my doubts about the venture. Now I understand it is a huge success, which is doubly reassuring because the strong yen has priced some made-in-Japan products out of foreign markets.

When I headed the air conditioner division, it had about 1,300 people, a fairly large operation. Yet it was small enough for quick feedback. When sales rose, I was delighted; if orders slowed, I felt the slack personally. Division morale was excellent. The staff responded to direction with alacrity, the way a winning ball club does or a platoon of crack troops. Each person felt his or her contribution counted. It was the happiest, most fulfilling time of my life.

2
The Bigness Syndrome

Until I was tapped for the presidency of Matsushita Electric, I had concentrated only on my division and knew little about the rest of the company. I attended the monthly directors' meetings, but I didn't pay much attention to overall corporate strategy. That was somebody else's problem.

Now, suddenly, I was to be responsible for everything. With my appointment scheduled to be officially confirmed by the board in February, I took a one-month cram course in Matsushita Electric. I pored over reports from every division, studied the balance sheets, and checked all the projections. As I worked my way through the mountain of paper, it slowly became clear to me that the company was in worse shape than I had imagined.

As far as the public knew, Matsushita Electric was a solid company. Matsushita executives bragged that it was the No. 1 home appliance maker in Japan, if not the world. My division had improved, and I had assumed the whole corporation was doing fairly well.

However, internal documents told a different story. We were in trouble, perhaps terminally ill. The problem wasn't just slow growth in home appliance sales, for Matsushita had become sluggish, overweight, myopic. Worst of all, the patient was so complacent that he didn't recognize his own mid-life crisis.

The consumer electronics market had reached saturation point. Japanese households were so full of appliances that there was nowhere to plug another one in. Video cassette recorders (VCRs), a relatively large item, were supposed to tide us over the postcolor television slump. But big-ticket products like that don't come along every year. Every industry hits a plateau after thirty years, much as a long-distance runner hits a "wall" at a certain point. After World War II, appliance makers first met pent-up demand and then inundated consumers with laborsaving or leisure products. Few people at Matsushita realized the Golden Age was over.

The prevalent attitude was, "Appliances are necessities, and since they wear out, we can count on steady replacement demand. Granted, the go-go days of rapid economic growth have ended, and we won't have 15 percent to 20 percent sales increases annually. But we will still have a certain level of demand."

Some people were optimistic about long-term prospects. The world's population is 4.1 billion, they said, of whom not more than 1 billion have appliances. Rising standards of living in developing countries would boost demand for Matsushita products. To men who had spent their whole career in consumer electronics, the future still looked rosy.

It was true that earnings and profits were still on the increase. As long as appliance sales rose, profits mounted and everything seemed fine. But if consumer electronics sales leveled off or fell, profits would plummet; the rest of the corporation couldn't take up the slack. Matsushita's size was misleading: it was flabby and vulnerable. We had to slim down and improve muscle tone.

In addition to these internal problems, the business environment was on the verge of two seminal changes. At home, Japan was becoming an information-based society. New growth was in data transmission and the microchip revolution. Abroad, global economic friction was intensifying and some production would have to be shifted offshore to get inside protectionist barriers.

To achieve new growth required huge capital outlays. Resources—money, people, and research and development (R&D) facilities—had to be allocated to the best advantage. In order to do this, we needed a solid management system. There was no time for leisurely adjustments. If I, a member of the board of directors, had not understood the crisis, then the average Matsushita employee couldn't be blamed for blissful ignorance. The essence of the danger was the disparity between earnings and profits: the operating profit ratio had been falling since 1969.

The Matsushita philosophy is that "the mission of an enterprise is to contribute to society." Profits reflect that contribution. In other words, an unprofitable company must not be doing work useful to society. Perhaps its products are lousy or maybe it is badly run. In any case, the balance sheet is both a managerial and moral scorecard.

When the board formally approved my promotion on February 18, 1977, I sounded a warning in my maiden speech that day: "Matsushita has become a great enterprise and our products are known all over the world. These laurels were well earned. But the question before us is, 'Are we doing enough today to sustain this fine record?'. . . In an emergency, the danger is obvious; when things are going well, it is difficult to sense trouble. The most dangerous mix is complacency in a crisis."

Complacency started at the top at Matsushita. The company had become a huge bureaucracy—layers of managers, countless meetings, and slow reaction time. It was a perfect example of the "bigness syndrome."

In 1977, of Matsushita's forty-eight operating divisions, only two had high profits: those producing electric irons and batteries, both in unglamorous, mature sectors of the economy. Profits were declining in all other divisions. I followed up my first speech by presenting these facts to the Monthly Meeting of Group Executives.

Divisions were usually ranked by sales volume. I decided to use a different criterion, the standard profit rate. Each division's performance was graded on an A to D scale. A means the division attained 90 percent or more; B, 60 percent to 90 percent; C, 40 percent to 60 percent; and D, below 40 percent. By this criterion, the electric iron and battery divisions were in category A; television and other large appliance divisions were in D. The figures shattered the illusion that the large divisions were the company's mainstay.

The reaction was swift and angry: "Profit isn't the only function of a corporation"; "We have to look five or ten years ahead at future profitability"; and "Our division is pouring money into research and development. Profit is low now, but the ratio will improve."

I stood my ground. If the so-called future-payoff expenditures had a precise justification, maybe I would have bought the arguments. Or if the speakers had described blockbuster products in the works, I would have been won over; all they talked about were abstract concepts. It struck me as ludicrous for someone to say he was "thinking of the future" when his present products didn't make money. If a company goes bankrupt, there is no future.

The gist of my remarks was that profit opportunities were being missed. Some divisions made money *and* invested in R&D for next-generation products. If some could do it, the others should be able to. Despite resentment from some division heads, I felt I had made my point.

The iron and battery divisions intrigued me. How were they able to turn in handsome profits in small, mature markets? I found complex factors were at work—an extraordinary level of know-how and effort. Let me describe both in greater detail, since they exemplify the special strength of Matsushita Electric's autonomous division system.

The Electric Iron Division

When the electric iron division was formed in 1927, there were a hundred companies making the product. Today there are four. In 1970, the domestic market reached 3.2 million units; the annual figure now is about 2.5 million. Matsushita Electric's iron division not only survived in a declining market but is the industry leader in new products and low-cost production.

The division is unique in several ways, such as its factory management system. Half the division's four hundred employees work in production, and they are divided into twelve teams, one for each stage of the manufacturing process. The teams consist of from five or six members to fifteen. Thus, a small division has been further compartmentalized. And each team forms an independent accounting unit.

The team leader "manages" the operation. Each team lays in a stock of semi-finished irons from the preceding group and processes these products, thereby adding value before sending them on to the next stage. Within the division this transfer is regarded as "sales." The team leader is responsible for reducing the cost of materials and other fixed expenses, and for expanding sales. Each team prepares monthly profit-and-loss statements. All Matsushita Electric divisions prepare financial statements, but the iron division has extended the process down to the team level.

The team leader, in fact all team members, have to think like managers. They are aware of market demand and fluctuations in basic material costs. These determine how their little company performs. The prices of parts, consumer demand, and wage rates all directly affect a team's work. Each member thinks like a division director; each person learns management skills daily on the job. The sales staff is equally management-conscious, regularly coming up with imaginative ideas to move the products. "The Iron Seminar" was a recent inspiration.

Millions of housewives today don't know how to iron clothes properly. The skill is not taught in high school home economics or adult education classes. A survey showed that 60 percent of housewives had never had instruction and were unsure if they were using the appliances correctly. One reason is that irons today are high-tech wonders, replete with accessories. The flatiron of yesteryear is an antique. Forty percent of the respondents said they wanted to learn the proper technique but had no one to teach them. Most clerks in home appliance stores were men or young women who themselves did not know how to iron.

The sales staff organized a five-hour how-to-iron course for retail clerks and called it "The Iron Seminar." Trainees were shown how an iron works—its parts and basic principles. Then they were taught technique, including how to iron shirt collars and trouser creases, and how to smooth out carpets. Graduates received a master ironer certificate from the division director.

Have you ever ironed a shirt? I am told that the collar is the hardest part. First you press the back to get the shape right. Then you turn the collar over and iron from the tips toward the middle, being careful to leave some slack. That is how professional laundry and dry cleaning shops do it. The technique is not easy or self-evident.

Retail stores initially refused to send personnel to attend the course, claiming they could not spare them, and anyway, the idea was half-baked. The division finally recruited ten reluctant students. Afterwards, the clerks admitted that ironing was more difficult than they had thought and that the course was beneficial. The clincher was higher sales at the participating shops: many customers bought new irons because trained demonstrators showed how to use them. Today, the iron division has two instructors who are in great demand for the course at appliance stores.

Recharging the Dry Battery Division

The dry battery division was established in 1931. In the early years its main products were flashlight and bicycle-light batteries. For several years after World War II, electric power was erratic, with frequent failures, and production of batteries rose steadily. In about 1952, however, power stoppages virtually ended, and bicycle makers installed a new battery-less light that worked from a dynamo on the front wheel. Total output of the battery industry reached 100 million units in 1955, and then began to fall. Matsushita's dry battery division was in a battle for survival.

If the division was closed, the employees faced transfers and separation from friends they had worked with for years. As Mark Twain said about hanging, adversity wonderously focuses the mind. Competing against other makers in a declining market—thinner slices of a shrinking pie—was a no-win situation. The division's answer was to increase overall demand by developing new products.

The first was an automatic pilot lighter for gas heaters and stoves. Most Japanese homes are equipped with gas water heaters in kitchens and bathrooms. Because of the danger of earthquakes, housewives turn off the pilot light when leaving the house and before retiring at night, but relighting the pilot with matches is a tiresome task. If the woman's hands are wet, the matches get damp and will not light. The hot ash from a match can also ruin clothes, and the match must be carefully put out and discarded to avoid causing a fire.

Matsushita's new lighter put an end to all these worries. About six inches long, you held it near the pilot cock, pressed the button, and the job was done.

The division sold 2 million lighters the first year. Each had two batteries that lasted three months; the lighter alone sold 16 million batteries in the year it was launched and 20 million units the next. The division turned out many more new products—from a burglar alarm system to a buzzer that signals when the bath water is hot.

In 1963, the division developed a high-performance "hyper-battery" with twice the power of conventional dry cells. This breakthrough led to new portable radios and tape recorders. In 1965, total battery production in Japan hit 1 billion units.

But success also created its own casualties. In the early 1960s, cash registers at appliance stores were ringing a happy refrain as consumers snapped up TVs, washing machines, and refrigerators. With expensive consumer durables selling well, dealers turned up their noses at low-profit-margin items like batteries. Shop owners didn't use point-of-purchase displays or restock on time. The dry cell division had to find new distribution channels.

Small items like batteries are a headache for retailers. Nevertheless, the division found outlets—sundries stores, stationery stores, gardening and fishing equipment stores, and record shops. These channels also inspired new products, such as battery-operated pencil sharpeners, microscopes with a battery-driven light, battery-powered insecticide dispensers and lawn mowers, a cleaner to remove static from records and an electric fishing float that used a lithium battery. In 1978, the dry cell division launched a sesame-seed grinder with an imaginative name-the-product publicity campaign that sold 1 million units that year. Among other new products was an electric firefly that blinked on and off, thanks to a luminous diode.

A pervasive sense of crisis had inspired the dry cell division to create these products and search for alternative sales outlets. Larger Matsushita divisions, however, were not afraid of being phased out. Managers tended to feel they would always muddle through and the staff was complacent.

At Matsushita Electric the president customarily announces management policy for the coming year at a meeting of seven thousand supervisory personnel on January 10. My first presentation was in 1978, after being in the post for eleven months.

I chose the theme "the starting point of management" because I feared Matsushita was losing sight of how it had become a great corporation. The gist of my remarks was that our sixty-year tradition of fine products was no guarantee of future success. There were countless cases of once-powerful companies that had collapsed like a house of cards. When internal weaknesses were ignored, they spread like a cancer, and one day the doors closed forever.

In a small company the production people and the sales staff are in face-to-face contact, they interact, and everyone feels that "your problem is my problem." Cooperation pulls them through hard times. A large company, however, is a complex maze where work is specialized and compartmentalized, and employees are engrossed in their own jobs. Centrifugal force must be controlled by coordination, but that causes conflicts of interest. On the other hand, failure to face the problem leads to chaos.

I appealed to all employees to recognize the danger. Then I discussed the criteria for a "good company." It is one whose products, policies, and employees have earned the community's respect. Every employee must be sensitive to what society expects from the enterprise, and must be constantly alert to changing values and needs. This is a corporation's moral duty. A company can survive only by doing work esteemed by society.

An enterprise must be a collection of quality people. Individual skill is important, of course, but teamwork translates into corporate power. Collective effort, that sense of working together, brings out the best in people and generates enthusiasm and ideas.

I made "revitalization" the goal for 1978. As I noted earlier, the enemy was complacency. To paraphrase Winston Churchill, I had not become president of Matsushita to preside over its gradual collapse. In keeping with the sixtieth anniversary, our slogan for the year emphasized determination worthy of our founding spirit. I tried to sound a clarion call against the pervasive conservatism and rekindle the original Matsushita dynamism in a bid for new corporate growth.

VCRs: The Big Decision

Several important decisions were pending when I took over the presidency. One concerned the distribution channels for air conditioners, which in 1976 were entering the stage of general diffusion among consumers. As head of the air conditioner division, I knew a shift from our sales company to Matsushita Electric's network of retail stores had been under study. Distribution was the purview of the sales department, and I had assumed they were implementing the new strategy.

But the plan was stalled because of vigorous objections from the sales company, which argued, "We built the air conditioner market, and now that our efforts are starting to pay off, you are going to pull the rug out from under us. We'll lose the best part of the market. Is this what loyalty means to Matsushita?" They had a point when air conditioners were very expensive, but if we were going to mass market them for home use, it made sense to utilize our retail network.

However, opposition was so strong that, swallowing my pride, I reversed my position and decided to stay with the sales company. The media made fun of my "unconditional surrender," calling it "the neophyte's blunder." Under the circumstances, I thought I was correct.

The most fateful decision of my first year concerned VCRs. There were two systems in existence—Matsushita's VHS and Sony's Betamax—and competition was fierce. Which one would dominate the huge U.S. market was the billion-dollar question. Zenith had already picked Betamax. If we couldn't get RCA to adopt VHS, the U.S. market was gone and, with it, Matsushita's future in VCRs.

Sony's VCR had a two-hour recording capacity, the longest at the time, which was why Zenith chose it. At Matsushita, we had a prototype two-hour VCR, but it was not ready for production. To sell in the United States, a VCR would have to be able to record long sports programs such as NFL football games. We were negotiating with RCA and knew they wanted a machine capable of longer recordings.

I bit the bullet and told RCA, "Matsushita can supply you with a four-hour VCR," and we signed a contract to deliver it. It was admittedly a rash gamble: we hadn't made a two-hour machine yet and didn't even have blueprints for a four-hour unit.

I explained the situation to our senior executives. "I know this is a dangerous move, but I want to go for it. If we back off, Matsushita is finished in VCRs. Despite the risks, we have a good chance of success. It's a tall order, but I want you to make that machine.

"The VCR division is going to be a living hell till August. Draw on the whole company for help. Everyone must realize how important this project is. Matsushita's fate is in the balance and I'm counting on you to get the job done."

We mobilized key people from other divisions, the research laboratory, and affiliated companies to help. They ate, drank, and slept four-hour VCRs. Miraculously, we met the contract deadline.

A brave decision, or one inevitable under the circumstances? Either way, the gamble paid off, with Betamax's defeat and a lucrative VCR market share for Matsushita.

The distribution and VCR decisions are particularly memorable because they came right after I became president. At the time, I thought decision making at Matsushita was too slow. Autonomous management was the lifeblood of the division system, and division directors were supposed to have full authority and responsibility. Some were more concerned, however, about pleasing headquarters than asserting their independence.

Matsushita Electric's head office had gotten too big, and its organization and functions often interfered in the divisions. Ironically, because of this meddling, units furthest from headquarters were the best-managed. Affiliated companies were more independent and better run than the divisions, and, among the divisions, the smaller, less glamorous ones that top management had little interest in performed better than the big ones that headquarters kept an eye on. The division system was instituted to invigorate small units functioning as part of a large organization, but, as each division expanded, it lost that flexibility and became unwieldy and bureaucratic.

Deciding Quickly

When asked the function of top management, I reply, "to make decisions." My job is to choose quickly from among alternatives, even if I make the wrong choice, because subordinates are waiting for a decision. "Even if I make the wrong choice" sounds like arrant nonsense, but mistakes can be spotted quickly and corrected. Executives who procrastinate from fear of making a mistake often miss golden opportunities and paralyze the organization. "Small is beautiful for a headquarters" was my slogan as president.

I realized the need for swift decision making early in my career when my own work was adversely affected by superiors who couldn't make up their minds. As a division director, and especially as president, I tried to make fast decisions. Otherwise, subordinates are stuck in limbo and the organization grinds to a halt.

The harder the problem, the more time senior executives need to consider it. Conversely, complex issues have far-reaching consequences and subordinates need a quick response, so I make the best choice open to me at the time. If I have assembled all the relevant data and thought the issue through, I have no regrets afterwards. However, you must have the courage to admit a mistake and rectify it, as I did with the air conditioner distribution problem.

A mountain climbing party suddenly beset by bad weather has to reconsider its route and make other plans. To continue or to go back? To take the route to the right or to the left? A group decision, where everybody expresses an opinion and the choice is a consensus based on compromise, is frequently wrong. An experienced climber should be in charge and make the decisions. This was the conclusion of a series of fascinating experiments on decision making at high altitudes conducted by Nagoya University's Research Institute of Environmental Medicine. Researchers simulated an altitude of twenty to twenty-three thousand feet in a low-pressure chamber. Seven mountain climbers were given a series of scenarios and asked to decide courses of action. The low atmospheric pressure made everyone a bit lightheaded; some behaved and spoke oddly. Nevertheless, the group leader functioned best and scored highest in the exercise because he had enormous experience and was accustomed to low-pressure conditions.

You can judge a baseball team's leadership when a pitcher gets in trouble. In a weak club, the infielders converge on the mound with conflicting advice: "Pitch to the batter." "No, walk him." The pitcher, confused and tentative, gives up a hit and that's the game. With a good team, the manager strides to the mound and unhesitatingly tells the pitcher what to do. Buoyed by the manager's confidence, the hurler usually retires the batter.

On a cold wind-swept mountain or in the late innings of a crucial ball game, decision by debate is the way to certain disaster. That holds true for business, too. When a fundamental policy choice must be made, a majority vote or consensus invites failure. If groupism worked, why have a president? Sometimes the top executive has to overrule his staff. For example, a staff-approved project may no longer be feasible. If a majority thinks a plan has a chance, you can be sure another company is already doing it. Rejecting staff proposals isolates the president, but the loneliness of command comes with the territory.

My method is not to consult with others when I make a decision. In Japan, consultation implies joint responsibility, with serious repercussions for everyone involved. Of course, I listen to relevant opinions, but I make the final choice. That means also taking any flak that follows. Unpopularity is also sometimes part of the territory.

A Present from Mr. Matsushita

When I took over in 1977, there were three operations groups—industrial equipment, wireless equipment, and home appliances—headed by executive vice presidents who stood between the president and the divisions. Although originally established to stimulate divisional independence, this redundant management layer in fact reduced divisional autonomy. After a year in office, I abolished it.

In doing so, I had to retire the three executive vice presidents. Although I was president, they were older than I, had had distinguished careers at Matsushita Electric, and had faithfully served Konosuke Matsushita for many years. Forcing them out was a painful decision. I took the problem to Mr. Matsushita.

"I plan to abolish the three main operations groups and retire the executive vice presidents. They are senior to me. . . ."

"Go ahead. If you think that should be done, then proceed. Who will tell them?"

"I prefer to do it."

The three men accepted my decision with admirable grace. It was a very awkward situation: the younger person cavalierly asking his seniors to step down. Their magnanimity made my task easier.

The media were not so kind and had a field day with me. Headlines screamed "YAMASHITA'S REVOLUTION," and the stories described me as a wrecker bent on destroying Matsushita's tradition. It was a drastic step that left me open to attack, I suppose. My intent had been the opposite, however: to revive the tradition of autonomous management and revitalize the company.

One day Mr. Matsushita brought a framed piece of calligraphy of two Chinese characters to my office. The first ideograph was *"dai"* for "great" or "large"; the second was *"nin"* (also read *shinobu*), which means "to endure" or "stoic patience." Mr. Matsushita's signature was on the drawing.

As president, I had done what I thought best for the company and called a spade a spade. Not all my moves met with Mr. Matsushita's approval; we sometimes differed over personnel and policy, giving rise to rumors of a falling out. Critics said I was impetuous and aloof, "the kind of man you don't feel comfortable with."

Mr. Matsushita was worried, I think, about the effect this talk might be having on me, and his present was a reminder that storms pass and patience is a virtue.

Handing me the calligraphy, he said, "I have the same characters on my wall. Remember when you look at this that I'm with you."

3
The Changing Face of Business

My first priority as president was to make Matsushita Electric's divisions profitable again by restoring their autonomy. This daunting task was complicated by the very uncertain business environment in the late 1970s. The first oil crisis in 1973 had ended rapid economic growth, and the effects of the second, including the yen's appreciation against the dollar, were ominously unclear.

Under such circumstances, a short-term outlook leaves you hostage to the morning headlines, always responding to new developments, and usually losing money with every panicky change. Matsushita operated according to the divisions' one-year plans: there was no mid-term or long-term planning. Overseas expansion, R&D, and enlarging a sales network must be based on the mid- and long-term outlook. I introduced a three-year plan that started from July 1978.

In 1981, I established a ten-year plan. The extraordinary changes in technology and the world economy required a far-sighted approach. To train people, you must have a sense of what the economy will look like a decade ahead. My objective was twofold: to look ahead at the kind of enterprise Matsushita would have to be in 1990 and identify specific measures to make that transition. I thought in nautical terms: a ship's captain with his course carefully set can survive stormy seas and reach port.

In the early 1980s, trade friction was becoming more serious, and Japan was accused of being a disruptive force. To keep Matsushita operations from becoming overly dependent on any one market, I set targets: 75 percent of production to be made in Japan (of which one-third would be for export) and 25 percent to be manufactured overseas.

The long-term plan revealed two interesting facets of Matsushita. Although still primarily centered on home appliances, we were evolving into a general electronics maker. Second, our move into the rapid-growth areas of semiconductors and industrial equipment was turning us into a multinational conglomerate. With clearer R&D priorities, we pushed ahead in the most promising fields.

In 1982, we stressed office automation (OA), robots, a camcorder with a built-in image-stabilization system, and videodisks. The next year we initiated special projects in the OA and the so-called new electronic media, which includes cable television, videotex, and communication services via telephone lines linked to personal computers. The research was mainly done at Matsushita laboratories, with help from various divisions and affiliated companies. Quick results convinced us that a cross-cutting approach—one that transcended divisional and corporate lines—enhanced our total capability.

In 1984, I initiated "Action 86," a three-year program with triple objectives: renewal of the business structure, enhancement of corporate strength, and expansion of overseas operations. I wanted to foster growth and tighten up management.

The three- and ten-year plans and "Action 86" were not sudden inspirations. They took shape slowly as I pondered Matsushita's future. Although no great business strategist, I thought a great deal about the factors that cause an enterprise and an industry to flourish or decline.

Many world-class corporations have slipped from prominence. *Fortune* magazine annually ranks manufacturers (excluding the oil industry) according to sales volume. In 1980, the top five U.S. companies were GM (General Motors), Ford, IBM (International Business Machines), GE (General Electric), and ITT (International Telephone and Telegraph). Twenty years earlier, GM and Ford were placed first and second, followed by GE, U.S. Steel, and Chrysler Corporation. IBM had been twentieth and ITT forty-second, so both had grown spectacularly in two decades. Of the top fifteen manufacturing companies in 1960, only seven were in that elite group in 1980, and of those seven, six had an after-tax profit rate above 4 percent.

Nikkei Business magazine publishes a similar analysis of Japanese enterprises. The editors track changes in the best one hundred companies, ranked according to sales volume. Of the top one hundred in 1923, only twenty were in that distinguished group in 1950. Furthermore, of the best one hundred in 1950, only thirty-four made the list in 1982. There was a 70 percent turnover in three decades.

Dynamic change characterizes Japanese industry. Of the one hundred best companies in 1950, fifty-seven were textile makers; by 1982, only four firms on the list were in textiles. Not only individual corporations but also whole industries are periodically shaken out.

Constant Reform

Evolution makes no exceptions in the marketplace. Even an enterprise highly successful with one product or line must constantly look for new opportunities. Being No. 1 in sales in an industry, as Matsushita was in home appliances, is a terrific accomplishment, but only constant, rigorous reform will keep you there. Choosing the safe course, the managerial equivalent of resting on one's laurels, destroys a company's vitality. Highly effective organizational structures must be radically revamped if the external environment changes. No configuration is perfect or eternal. Adapt or fail is the rule of the marketplace.

Occasionally taking unconventional action shakes up an organization. People set in their ways need to be jolted now and then. Rules are made to be followed, but a confident leader knows when to ignore custom or established policy. The timid executive who says "There's no precedent!" and sticks to the rules ends up in bankruptcy court.

New leadership often requires different organizational arrangements. The newcomer's work style or priorities may be incompatible with existing structures. There are always naysayers, however, who regard the organization chart as holy writ.

When a company is losing money, it's easy to carry out changes. Otherwise, the mentality is, "If it isn't broken, don't fix it." A crisis may be only a few months away, but myopic people can't see it. As president, I wanted to change some operations radically. I tried to gain assent by carefully explaining the need for reform, using statistics for the "quants," who love quantitative data, and other methods for those less mathematically inclined.

At Matsushita Electric, every month we hold a joint meeting of group executives, which is attended by about three hundred persons. I wanted candid discussion at these meetings, so I told the participants to cut out the hot air and exaggerated claims. "Let's be completely honest here," I said and insisted that comments be based on data, analysis, and hard information. Subordinates will withhold essential information from a CEO if they think he prefers an upbeat tone. Middle managers don't want to disclose anything that reflects adversely on themselves or their section, so bad news tends to stop at this level. "I want to know what is going on, including problems," I said. "This meeting is pointless if I'm given only sugarcoated reports." I was to have to repeat the injunction many times.

Some subordinates urged me not to rock the boat: "If the proposed changes improve operations, then people will say, 'Yamashita was right.' But what if, because of faulty estimates or incomplete data, your innovations fail? Critics will say, 'We warned you. Our worst fears have been confirmed.' Employee morale will plummet. Failure could destroy your credibility."

There was strong opposition to my program and I had to avoid mistakes at all costs, of course. That was precisely why I needed honest, accurate information as a basis for decision making.

R&D: The Lifeblood of a Company

Kenya wanted to increase the number of tourists visiting a wildlife preserve in Nairobi. Officials decided to feed the lions instead of allowing them to fend for themselves. With a regular feeding time, they thought, the park could guarantee that visitors would see the majestic animals and attendance would rise.

As a result, however, they soon saw that the lions couldn't hunt for themselves. Although lions are believed to be so strong and fast that they easily dominate other animals, it is the females that actually do most of the hunting and they are relatively slow runners. So lionesses must keep physically fit. It takes all their agility and cunning to stalk and corner prey, and intended victims either flee or turn and fight with their horns and claws.

In a short while, the park's veterinary hospital was full of wounded lions, and the experiment was called off. Not having to forage for food had made the lions slow and careless and had sapped their strength. It was the constant struggle for survival that had made them the "king of the beasts."

A similar fate can befall corporations: a successful company can soon be a docile, weak pussycat. The CEO must keep it lean and fast, always on the hunt. Technological innovation is the corporate equivalent of a lion's brute strength, long canine teeth, and sharp claws. A company feasts on its technological breakthroughs, but if management complacently dotes on these triumphs, it soon becomes prey for others. The bleached bones of many once-powerful companies show that your best asset can also become a liability.

Shortly after becoming president, I took charge of the corporate engineering division. Matsushita's future depended on fairly long-range R&D planning. Although our research facilities were doing good work, the emphasis was on the short-term, or next year's products, and there was a bias in favor of consumer electronics.

Today, technological progress is moving so rapidly that products are soon outdated. Sometimes a technical breakthrough will even bury an entire craft. Spring-driven clocks and watches are a good example.

Japanese clocks made their mark on the world in 1964, when quartz-crystal clocks were designated the official timepieces of the Tokyo Olympics, an honor previously monopolized by the Swiss. Although scientific institutes and broadcasting stations had relied on quartz-crystal clocks for many years, they were too expensive, large, and heavy for general use. The 1964 model clocks used in the Olympics represented a revolutionary innovation. They weighed three kilograms and were easier to operate than earlier models, but they were still heavy and cumbersome compared to today's clocks. However, the Olympics earned Japanese quartz-crystal clocks a reputation for accuracy, and sales took off. As quartz-crystal clocks were refined and made smaller, the price steadily dropped. Soon it was hard to find an old-fashioned spring-driven clock. In 1975, quartz-crystal clocks had had only a 10 percent market share; by 1985, that had become more than 80 percent.

Quartz-crystal clocks and watches are not only more accurate but they are virtually defect-free because of the simplicity of their design. In the old days, repairing finely engineered, precision timepieces was a skilled craft. Quartz-crystal clocks made that profession redundant. In two decades the watchmaking industry as a whole has changed enormously.

Today it is centered, by volume, in Hong Kong (40 percent), Japan (20 percent), and Switzerland (6 percent). Hong Kong leads in manufacturing inexpensive models, followed by Japan; Switzerland makes mainly luxury items and watch-accessory combinations that require skilled craftsmanship. The market is polarized into the cheap and the luxury sectors.

The Japanese-language typewriter is another example of an industry destroyed by new technology—word processors. Although the Japanese-language typewriter was never as popular as its Western counterpart, before the advent of word processors in 1981 makers shipped about 130,000 machines annually, mainly to printers, schools, and companies. By 1985, sales were down to 65,000 units, and in 1986 only 10,000 machines were sold.

The first word processors sold for ¥1.6 million in 1981. The price fell to ¥1 million the next year, and then in stages to ¥700,000 and ¥400,000. As soon as the price hit ¥120,000 in 1985, they became popular for personal and home use. Today, at Akihabara, Tokyo's discount electronics mecca, word processors sell for ¥40,000 or less.

Japanese-language typewriters were knocked out of the market by these low prices, the manufacturers have gone out of business, and the typists who used the machines had to learn new skills. Managers beware: the only defense against technological innovation is farsighted R&D.

In the 1950s, every Japanese family wanted three appliances—a black-and-white TV, a refrigerator, and a washing machine. The second wave of labor-saving devices included vacuum cleaners and automatic rice cookers, which were followed by home air conditioners and microwave ovens. Mesmerized by success, appliance makers dreamed of an endless stream of new gadgets. At Matsushita Electric, five decades of making appliances had institutionalized an R&D bias in favor of improving existing products. But no matter how many minor changes engineers come up with for refrigerators and washing machines, or what clever spinoff products they devise, it's impossible to achieve significant product differentiation. Marketing becomes crucial, and a huge retail network like Matsushita's is highly advantageous. A company, however, may feel too secure. The attitude at Matsushita was, "Our nationwide retail outlets make us invincible in consumer electronics. All we have to do is get new items into the stores."

Learning from 3M

3M, the famous U.S. manufacturer, has a "25 percent policy": one-quarter of sales in each division must be from products that didn't exist five years earlier. It is a remarkable commitment to constant innovation.

Each division and sector at 3M has its own laboratory; in addition, there is a central laboratory accessible to the entire company. The three organizational levels work in different time frames: divisions—five years ahead; sectors—ten years in the future; and central—ten to twenty years into the unknown.

Divisions at 3M have great latitude. A project, for example, to turn a laboratory discovery into commercial products may have a $2 million budget. The division may allocate the funds as it wishes. However, the project must show a profit within three years or be terminated.

Anyone at 3M can propose new projects. An engineer, let's call him Smith, first goes to his division chief. If the boss rejects his idea, Smith can take it to another division. The "25 percent policy" puts all division chiefs on the lookout for new products, so Smith has a good chance of finding support somewhere. When an idea is accepted, a new venture team is formed of volunteers from different disciplines who can return to their home division if the project fails. These task forces work like whirling dervishes because they are true believers. 3M's corporate culture is unusually supportive of fresh thinking and innovation. It seems no Japanese company can match its commitment to creativity.

3M's personnel policy has a Japanese flavor. Turnover is low and family members are included in company social events. Some Japanese writers like to contrast management styles: the cold, rational methods of U.S. companies versus the affective, people-centered approach of Japanese firms. But the best-run U.S. corporations have much in common with Japanese companies.

Several years ago, Sherwood L. Fawcett, president of the Battelle Memorial Institute, the world's largest nonprofit scientific organization, gave a lecture in Japan. Explaining how his institute functions, Fawcett said it invests three years or five years in a project without knowing whether the project will succeed or not. Great patience is necessary, he said, likening that waiting period to "walking through the valley of the shadow of death." How true! The long march to a new product is an act of faith and courage.

Integrated Circuits Take Off

In 1977, the hottest products in the electrical machinery and appliance industry were computers and color TVs, worth about ¥700 billion, followed by tape recorders, stereos, and air conditioners. The strength of these five items led many appliance executives to assume continued expansion in this sector. However, by 1984, computer sales had soared, and two newcomers, semiconductors and VCRs, were second and third, respectively, with sales above ¥2 trillion each. Although appliances still made money, if Matsushita had neglected other fields, it would have registered little growth for the period.

Matsushita executives realized that times were changing, but they had difficulty shifting gears. Since sales figures had not actually fallen, many tended to be optimistic about the future of appliances and refused to see the storm clouds on the horizon.

Top Five Electrical Machinery/Appliances
(Unit: ¥ million)

Rank	1964 Product	Sales	1977 Product	Sales	1984 Product	Sales
1	B/w TVs	192,480	Computers	719,274	Computers	2,941,884
2	Refrig- erators	119,738	Color TVs	700,805	Semi- conductors	2,584,239
3	Radios	98,363	Tape recorders	663,155	VCRs	2,090,210
4	Washing machines	42,928	Stereos	522,912	Color TVs	775,761
5	Stereos	33,058	Air con- ditioners	329,003	Air con- ditioners	618,233

Source: Compiled from Ministry of International Trade and Industry Statistics.

There was also the pull of the past: Matsushita had always been an appliance maker, so a change signified a break with tradition.

Another factor that slowed Matsushita's move into personal computers and semiconductors was that the company had withdrawn from the mainframe market in 1964. Yet to be constrained by that decision in the late 1970s meant being shut out of the hottest growth sectors.

The decision to withdraw was correct, in my opinion. At that time, Matsushita didn't have the resources to compete in the mainframe market. Concentrating on consumer electronics, the fastest-growth sector, made the company the industry leader. But it was a different ballgame in the late 1970s, and computer and semiconductor sales were in a different league from home appliances. Matsushita's own appliances now used semiconductors, for example. To ignore the integrated circuit (IC) would have been like the captain of the *Titanic* saying, "It's only an iceberg."

I poured people and money into semiconductors, convinced that we had to make the move while there was still time. But human nature is curious. Precisely because Matsushita's appliance sales were still strong, nobody had a sense of urgency. Some managers will always think, "Why chase other companies in an expensive, unfamiliar sector?" and to convince these skeptics takes precious time. When nine out of ten people are opposed to an idea, it is just about the right moment to push ahead. By the time nine out of ten understand that a company is in danger, you're doomed.

Hitachi, NEC, Fujitsu, Toshiba, and several other companies already had a head start in IC-based information technology. We had to become a major player, and that meant an aggressive catch-up strategy. I gave this sector top priority in allocating resources. I asked the new electronic media, office automation, and semiconductor divisions to boost sales by 20 percent annually.

ICs were driving the technological revolution. New products in which chips were a major cost component appeared almost daily. If we could make smaller, better, and cheaper ICs, we could cut product prices dramatically. For example, chips represented 60 percent of the materials cost of word processors and 30 percent of VCRs. Lowering IC prices would make both products cheaper. It was a virtuous circle: lower prices would lead to more sales, which would permit mass production and economies of scale.

Customers who bought word processors when they were still expensive often complained, "I should have waited a little longer. I paid too much!" They have my sympathy because I paid ¥300,000 for my own machine. However, there is solace in the thought that I enjoyed the benefits of a word processor earlier than people who waited for the price to come down. I consider the "exorbitant price" a contribution to the advancement of technology.

The IC revolution had a similar impact on electronic calculators. The first models marketed by Sharp sold for ¥600,000, which was about the price of a small car at the time.

Now you can buy one for ¥2,000 or less, and replace it almost as readily as a disposable lighter.

Human beings need time to become accustomed to any technology or system, but it was very difficult to keep pace with ICs as their memory capacity quadrupled in three years. New products were brought out constantly and prices fell sharply. But attempting to restrain technological change—to give us all a breathing space—would be misguided. Engineers are assiduously expanding scientific knowledge. Asking them to "take a break" would halt progress. There is no turning back: R&D teams deserve the green light.

Now, there is intense competition to develop very large-scale integrated (VLSI) memory chips. The 256-kilobit chip is already outdated; we will soon have one-megabit and four- to sixteen-megabit chips. These powerful chips will probably make voice-activated word processors and interpreting machines feasible within a decade.

More powerful chips enabled engineers to downsize computers, and the ICs were designed into home appliances. Microprocessor units (MPUs) have added new features to refrigerators and washing machines. MPUs have also created new markets. For example, hotel rooms now have self-service refrigerators that instantly record on a guest's bill what he or she has removed. There would have been little value added for Matsushita in just making the refrigerator shell; we also had to manufacture the IC-driven microprocessing unit. A company Matsushita's size couldn't be dependent on outside suppliers for ICs.

In the information age, computers and semiconductors are the major growth sectors, a development that Matsushita was late in appreciating. Unless we moved quickly, the future was grim. "Action 86" set the priorities and focused our energies. It called for heavy investment of people, facilities, and money in the information sector. Half-measures wouldn't work; neither would new priorities squeezed into the old management matrix. We had to strengthen Matsushita management and simultaneously control the appliance side and the new information side. Our expertise and marketing strength was in consumer electronics, where rising sales were not to be expected. We had to increase profits without growth. I was taking the corporation into dangerous, uncharted seas, but it was the only way to escape the doldrums.

People and Technology

Technology is the essence of manufacturing. Although it has made the industrialized nations affluent, the price has often been destruction of the environment and alienation—the loss of a human touch in products and services.

We need perspective and balance in our lives lest technology intrude and dominate. Matsushita recently introduced TV conferences between Osaka and Tokyo. Managers in both cities can see each other on the screen while discussing a problem. But these conferences are rarely conclusive. Afterwards, an executive usually tells me he must go to Tokyo. When I ask why, since the issue was supposedly wrapped up in the TV conference, he says, "Well, there is one complicated point I want to talk over." People prefer face-to-face contact when they make important decisions. They want to look the other person in the eye, check his attitude, get a feel for his energy level. You can't do that in TV conferences, at least not yet.

If TV conferences were a panacea, President Ronald Reagan and General Secretary Mikhail Gorbachev wouldn't have to hold summit meetings such as the one that took place in Reykjavik, Iceland. They could talk to each other from the White House and the Kremlin, and the whole world could tune in to the superpower dialogue. But national leaders meet because personal contact is the only way to take each other's measure.

When the well-known artist Keiichi Makino painted my portrait several years ago, I assumed he would do it from photographs, but he came to see me several times. "I cannot work from photos," Makino said. "They don't show personality. You might think a TV conference with the subject would be sufficient. The person is animated, talking, and moving, and an artist should be able to catch the right expression and attitude. But TV is no good either."

People accustomed to writing memos and letters by hand find it difficult to express themselves on a word processor, perhaps because of an unconscious resistance to the machine, which is so impersonal compared with the feel of pen and paper. I would have thought a love letter had to be handwritten. But word processor aficionados say they type them, too! The Romeos do sign their names, however. Some word-processor addicts occasionally write letters by hand just for the pleasure of holding a brush. We need to balance impersonal technology with a personal, an emotional, touch. This is why, I think, Westerners write their signatures on a typed letter.

A career woman once told me that from Monday to Friday she feeds her family frozen foods or take-out dishes purchased on the way home. On weekends, however, she always fixes regular meals and does everything by hand, from slicing the cucumbers to deep-frying the tempura. It satisfies her need for both a balanced diet and a well-rounded lifestyle.

Life is a seesaw ride, a series of ups and downs, victories and defeats. We have to ameliorate those swings and keep a rhythm in our lives.

Stepping Down

In retrospect, I am convinced that "Action 86" was good for Matsushita. As I've indicated, many of my colleagues misunderstood my objectives and were opposed to it, and the doubting Thomases said, "Why turn the company upside down when the profit picture is still good?" Or, "The information and new electronic media sectors are Matsushita's weak point. We may fail badly." Or, "Are we getting out of appliances altogether? What will happen to our retailers?"

Nevertheless, as we implemented the program, the complaints stopped. Matsushita's transformation was on track. Interestingly, even the managers of the appliance divisions, prompted partly by anger at my calling their sector "mature," worked harder to turn out new products and raise sales. Our offshore operations, too, were under active review. In 1984, the first year of "Action 86," the yen suddenly began to appreciate against the dollar, and this spurred our efforts to diversify overseas.

The transition was particularly tough on the managers of the new sectors because Matsushita was far behind and inexperienced. The semiconductor division invested heavily in research. In October 1985, Matsushita Electronics opened a laboratory in Kyoto and the next month Matsushita Electric set up a semiconductor research center. The former concentrated on general-purpose ICs while the latter worked on memory chips for future products. The two facilities cost a total of ¥40 billion, and, to my delight, we are already seeing the payoff.

The greatest achievement of "Action 86" was to convince Matsushita employees that the company had to change. Younger people joined the ranks of management, bringing with them an appreciation of the technocratic society of the future.

"Action 86" was scheduled to end in November 1986. Then Matsushita would be ready for the next stage, I thought, and that should be handled by my successor. It seemed advisable to make the change early so the next man would benefit from the reform program's momentum, just as in a relay race both runners should be going full speed when the baton is passed. Fortunately, Executive Vice President Akio Tanii had been deeply involved in "Action 86" and all company operations. In early 1985, I decided to retire as of February 1986.

Each January 10, the president of Matsushita outlines that year's goals, attempting to dramatize them in a slogan. A company-wide committee drafts several catch phrases for him to choose from. I often found that one was perfect. The slogans for my nine years at the helm were:

- 1978: Within the Spirit in Which Our Company Was Founded, We Should Be Positive and Aggressive.
- 1979: Reach for the Pinnacle.
- 1980: React Quickly. Respond Wisely.
- 1981: In the 50th Year of "Meichi" (Recognition of the Corporate Mission), Let Us Prove Our Ability to the Fullest Extent.
- 1982: Link the World Together with All Our Hearts and Technology.
- 1983: Build Strength into Our Products.
- 1984: Build Today—Challenge Tomorrow.
- 1985: Create the Future.
- 1986: Move Forward in Harmony with the World.

The slogans are short, but at least they are easy to remember. Some people at Matsushita said they typified me. In any case, they show my emphasis in the early years on revitalizing Matsushita, whereas in the later period they focused on international trade. Concern for the company's future competitiveness was a constant theme.

4
Adversity Builds Character

Every manager knows that utilizing people properly is the most difficult aspect of business, but it remains an elusive art. Konosuke Matsushita once gave me some good advice.

Many years back, an incompetent superior had driven me to the end of my tether and I complained to Mr. Matsushita: "I can't do my job. And it's not only me. Everyone's work has been affected."

He said, "Even if all our managers were paragons of moral uprightness, that wouldn't necessarily make them good businessmen. Your boss has shortcomings, sure, but he also has strengths. Rather than concentrate on his defects, you had better recognize his talents."

Emphasis on a person's good qualities was the heart of Mr. Matsushita's philosophy of personal growth, both as citizens and businessmen. It all depends on how you look at other people. He used to tell us, "Instead of correcting an employee's inadequacies, put your efforts into getting the most out of his skills."

It's much easier to capitalize on people's talents than to worry about their bad habits. As his skills improve, an imperfect employee adds a new dimension. A flawed person can be likable, whereas the paragon is hard to take.

I didn't suddenly see my boss in a different light because of

55

Mr. Matsushita's advice. I was still very frustrated. I'm no saint and I couldn't change my attitude so easily. But gradually I realized Mr. Matsushita's philosophy required me to become a better person, more magnanimous and tolerant of shortcomings in others. The inability to see another person's good points showed my own immaturity.

Parents face the same challenge. Every child has many admirable idiosyncrasies, but we judge them on standardized academic performance—on grades or class standing. We don't look for their individual talents. So-called norms are a poor way of evaluating people. There are hundreds of yardsticks by which this incredibly complex being called *Homo sapiens* should be assessed. Yet we tend to use the easiest, most obvious criterion: in the business world, that is educational background—the prestige of the college a person graduated from.

Deciding a child's future on the basis of multiple-answer test scores or an employee's career according to the college he attended is terribly unfair. Parents and supervisors must keep an open mind. This requires personal maturity and growth, an ability to size up and relate to people.

An enterprise needs all kinds of people because diversity ensures an array of talents. Scientists who study the interaction of microbes report that a very small amount of a foul-smelling element brings out the fragrance in perfume and gives soy sauce its pleasant aroma. It's almost as if one bad apple improves the whole barrel. Similarly, the walls of Japan's famous old castle moats were built by fitting different-sized, irregularly shaped stones together. This technique made them indestructible.

It's impossible to run a complex corporation with one-dimensional people, no matter how intelligent they are. To paraphrase Mr. Matsushita, sages can't necessarily meet a payroll. Recruiting only strong personalities and can-do go-getters won't make a workplace function. Some jobs are better suited to quiet, introverted personality types. You have to match tasks to the employees' skills: round pegs in round holes.

Once you have the right people in the right jobs, it's up to the corporate culture to get the maximum effort from them.

In a symphony orchestra, the French horn and viola rarely play the main melody and they are not so pleasing when played solo. They support the other instruments, however, to create a beautiful harmony. Musicians say practicing alone is boring, but the exhilaration of performing with a full orchestra and being part of that splendid sound compensates for the routine drudgery.

A growing company is a complicated organization somewhat like a symphony orchestra. Centrifugal force pulls sections in different directions. Gaps open between divisions, a no-man's land of products or technology that no one is responsible for. Employees cannot answer a customer's question, for example, unless it is about a matter their section handles; or worse yet, they may not even know where to refer it. The larger the company, the greater the possibility things will fall between the cracks.

These are an organization's windows of vulnerability. Strangely enough, work at the cracks in between parts of a company is often extremely important. In a flexible, dynamic organization, someone will cover this area, making whatever ad hoc adjustments are necessary. Creating that teamwork is like getting orchestra musicians to play well together. But in a rigid, conservative organization, no one steps into the void. Sections are afraid of getting involved, of making a mistake. Both parties at the edge of the cracks back off. Suddenly there is an opening a rival can exploit.

The fault lies less in organizational structure than with the people who are running the show. Some immerse themselves completely in their division and forget it's only one part of a larger entity. Others get bogged down in their own jobs and resist change or alternative ways of doing things. People of a third type live in their own little world and resent "interference" from others. This type is the hardest to deal with.

As such employees proliferate, the organization loses its original efficiency and vitality.

Conversely, if employees liaise with other divisions, think in cooperative terms, and get on with the work regardless of the organizational chart, then an enterprise remains dynamic. The creative juices flow and the job gets done. The iron and dry battery divisions exemplify this at Matsushita Electric. The employees understand not only their small unit but the big picture as well. Teamwork is second nature. Feuding with another division is as much an anathema as an argument with a good friend.

The battery division has factories in Osaka, Tsujido near Yokohama, Nagoya, and Kyushu. The last two each have about thirty employees and only one production line, incredibly small operations by Matsushita standards. Conventional wisdom says they are uneconomical and should be absorbed by the Osaka or Tsujido plants, and I used to wonder why we kept them open.

During a business trip to Kyushu, I made a point of visiting the battery factory there. The building dates from 1943 and reminded me of the back-alley subcontracting workshops you find in big cities. The foreman explained their operations: "We make batteries for Kyushu. Our costs must be lower than the cost of producing and shipping batteries from Osaka. That's our bottom line." During the preceding five-year period, the work force had fallen from forty to thirty-two while production had risen 30 percent. Costs had been lowered by not replacing retirees, and yet the factory still managed to boost output. The average worker was forty-three years of age, considerably older than at other Matsushita facilities, and had been with the company for twenty-three years. Despite the ancient building and aging employees, plant performance compared favorably with that of the ultramodern Osaka factory.

At the Nagoya factory, there were twenty-eight employees and the average age was thirty-seven. The building was constructed in 1933! Nevertheless, through sheer ingenuity the workers had kept production up to par. They had curved the single assembly line, for example, so that each person could do two different tasks. All the employees could handle any job; instead of narrow specialists they were all Renaissance men. And they were goal-oriented: there were specific production targets for each individual, each work group, and for the factory as a whole. Matsushita executives had considered closing the Nagoya factory and shifting production to Tsujido three times. On each occasion, a review showed the plant was highly efficient and it was left alone.

Nearly all the Nagoya workers would have had to quit Matsushita if production was shifted to Tsujido. They had local roots, and for family reasons relocation would be out of the question. They understood that if productivity slipped, the plant would be closed.

Matsushita has been making batteries for sixty years, and I thought maximum efficiency had been reached, but the Kyushu and Nagoya employees, whose average age is over forty, are still improving the operation. There is nothing pathetic, no nursing-home atmosphere in these factories. The workers are upbeat and get along together better than workers at state-of-the-art facilities.

Good people and effort count for more than equipment. The ideal combination is employees with diverse skills united by a common goal and doing their best for the company. And they should be self-motivated, not constantly pushed by management.

The Miracle Drug of Productivity: Personnel Shifts

Each month at Matsushita there is an informal get-together with retiring employees, a combination farewell party and debriefing session. I always asked them to speak frankly, since it was their last day with us, but most were deferentially reticent. One seemingly candid man said, "I am very happy that I was able to do the same job for forty years without being transferred to other assignments." He probably had been quite content, but what he said distressed me. If he had done other kinds of work and developed multiple skills, he would have been better prepared for retirement. I felt sorry for him.

It would be terrible if a retiree had said, "I wasted my life working for Matsushita." Fortunately, that never happened. But I wanted our people to have a variety of work experiences because that is how you discover your own potential. It was important to me that employees be motivated, have a sense that they are performing a useful function, and enjoy their work. The best way to keep people alert and interested is by personnel transfers.

In a rigid, ossified organization many employees spend their entire careers in one division. They lose their zest for new and difficult assignments. Specialization was all right perhaps when an employee worked on only one product, TV, for example. But today there are many system products—interrelated spin-offs such as VCRs and personal computers linked to TV, and narrow specialization is a handicap. Management needs employees with a breadth of interests, contacts, and experience. Career development has to encourage that personal growth.

Personnel shifts revitalize an organization. As president, I pushed interdivisional transfers and exchanges. Critics said I moved people around too much, but I believe the policy was correct. Starting in 1978, about three thousand employees were shifted annually, and in the last years of my tenure the figure rose to almost four thousand. It was an internal migration: excluding female employees, about 14 percent to 15 percent of our work force was involved.

Usually you can learn a job thoroughly in five years and then you coast. The first three years you are completely absorbed; there is no time to think creatively. In the next two years, you build on that experience, adding your own know-how and innovations. You're still motivated and alert. But after five years, the job is too easy. No longer intellectually stimulated, you stop discovering better ways to do things. You become a "learned fool," a specialist who knows everything about his job and little about anything else. A successful project can be a trap. You're the expert; no one can beat you. Your little world is too comfortable to leave.

Most of that knowledge and experience is irrelevant when you switch jobs. That's why it takes courage to leave the nest. But facing a new challenge gets the adrenalin flowing. You think faster and there is a spring in your step. New surroundings and associates are a Fountain of Youth, until age forty at least. After that, some people find it impossible to adjust to new duties. Transfers are most effective up to about age thirty-five. My goal was to have younger employees work in at least three different jobs before they reached the manager level.

Although some transfers, of course, are made because a person is not working out or giving a below-average performance, the primary rationale is to enable people to demonstrate their hidden talents. Lateral transfers widen the individual's perspective and tap latent skills while raising creativity in the divisions by injecting ideas and know-how. The results are often amazing. The infusion of new thinking and energy stimulates other personnel to try harder; the ripple effect invigorates the whole company. Transfers are also the miracle cure for organizational fatigue.

Many people who were initially reluctant to move were later thankful. One staff-level employee deeply resented a posting to another division. Three years later he told me, "If I had stayed in my former job, I would have been blissfully ignorant. The transfer opened my eyes to entirely different methods."

I wish I had a thousand yen for every time I heard, "I'm not suited for that kind of job." Although the individual's opinion has to be taken into consideration, a surprising number of people don't know what kind of work they would be good at. As division director, I wanted to reassign a design engineer, let's call him Watanabe, to a sales position that required a technical background. Watanabe refused: "I am not good at talking to people and could not work in sales. Please let me stay in design. If ordered to take the job, with all due respect, I will have to resign." He meant it, too, so I left him with his blueprints. His rationale was flawed, however. An ability to deal with people—human relations—is more important in business than eloquence. Some cantankerous customers are very demanding. You can't talk your way into their confidence. Many successful salesmen will never win a toastmaster's prize. In fact, glibness puts clients on their guard. It's not mellifluous words but whether you honor what you say that counts. When customers feel, "I can trust him," the orders follow.

Several years after Watanabe refused the transfer, Matsushita decided to build the air conditioner factory in Malaysia that I mentioned earlier, and we needed an engineer to oversee the construction. The best-qualified person was Watanabe, and I called him in.

"You turned down that sales job a few years back, but I'd like you to be the chief engineer for the factory we're building in Malaysia," I said.

"No thank you. I am not good at explaining things or supervising people. I have trouble with the Japanese: how could I work with Malaysians?" he replied.

"Don't worry about English or language problems. The local construction workers will only speak Malaysian and you only speak Japanese. Since you can't communicate with one another anyway, just talk in Japanese. I'll give you an assistant who will interpret and handle all negotiations. I really need your help on this," I said.

But Watanabe still refused to go. I talked to him several times over the next few weeks and finally, just when I was about to ask someone else, he agreed. A year later I visited him in Malaysia and found a changed man. The construction was on schedule and the Malaysians obviously respected him. Watanabe had established excellent rapport and teamwork. Many people like Watanabe are afraid to try a new job. But the Malaysia assignment showed him he had managerial ability. My advice is never take yourself for granted.

Failure Is the Best Teacher

Personal growth is directly proportionate to hard-earned experience and setbacks. Adversity builds character and the mental toughness to ignore minor irritations and keep a sense of proportion. Conversely, when the man who has always had smooth sailing founders for the first time, he is often overwhelmed.

There is a difference, however, between a minor setback and a major blunder. My point is not that employees should recklessly endanger their careers but that they shouldn't be afraid of making mistakes. In Japanese swordsmanship, a cut on the arm or shoulder is called a *mukō kizu*, as opposed to a mortal wound in the stomach or back. Anyone can stand a few *mukō kizu* on their record, though a major error can be fatal.

In 1984, I looked into Sumitomo Bank's personnel system to find out what made it such a dynamic outfit. The salient factors turned out to be quality leadership at the top and a fair personnel evaluation system, neither too lenient nor too severe. Board chairman Ichiro Isoda's dictum, "Don't be afraid of *mukō kizu*," guided personnel ratings, and initiative and reasonable risk-taking were encouraged. Isoda didn't mean, "Failure doesn't matter." A million dollar slip-up is a disaster even for a world-class bank, but he recognized that no one is perfect and fear of failure can destroy élan.

Some readers may object that I seem to be saying that failure is a precondition for success, as if an unblemished record was somehow disqualifying. Leaving aside what constitutes success, I think it is extremely important that managers in senior positions have experienced frustration and setbacks. An executive who hasn't suffered "the slings and arrows of outrageous fortune" can't empathize with the ordeals of others. It was my practice to give tough assignments to people I thought had a bright future with Matsushita so they could show their ability under pressure.

The downside to this policy is that if the subordinate doesn't understand the reason for his assignment, he may feel aggrieved and lose his motivation. A supervisor has to keep an eye on how the transferee is doing or occasionally offer some advice.

There are two approaches to motivating people: to make the employee more valuable to the company or to help him achieve his full potential. The latter is more effective because employees will not respond if the corporation's interests are put first. But people who are given the opportunity to make full use of all their abilities enjoy their work. It's management's job to channel that drive into profits.

I often say, "There is a lifetime commitment involved, so it's essential that the individual's goals be in line with those of the company. Identity of purpose is the ideal." It's a fortunate person, indeed, whose job perfectly accords with his aspirations. But in the "real world," people rarely get exactly the job they want. Most men and women are doing tasks they consider boring or beneath them. You can't run a company by letting the staff do only what interests them.

The challenge is to enjoy work we don't feel suited for. In a sense, whether you like a job or not is irrelevant. What counts is to try hard and get a sense of accomplishment from that effort. This builds confidence.

Interpersonal relations often determine job satisfaction. A great assignment can be soured by unpleasant working conditions or a bad boss. On the other hand, in an amicable environment employees will put up with hardship and long hours. One way supervisors can create that environment is to recognize,

Above: Konosuke Matsushita, founder and executive advisor of Matsu-shita Electric Industrial Co., Ltd., with the calligraphy he gave to the author, reading *dai-nin*, which means "great patience."

Below: The author with former president Masaharu Matsushita at a press conference held on January 18, 1977, to announce his presidency.

The Osaka headquarters of Matsushita Electric.

The Central Research Laboratory of Matsushita Electric in Osaka.

The company was founded in 1918 in this house (*above*), later made into the Museum of History of Matsushita Electric (*right*).

The author at the electric iron division (*above*) and the dry battery division (*below*).

Above: Executive Vice President (later President) Akio Tanii in September 1983, explaining the program called "Action 86."

Below: Recent products from Matsushita: (*above left*) a compact video camcorder; (*above right*) a laptop word processor with a 48-dot printer; (*below left*) the Panacom M 32-bit personal computer; (*below right*) a high-quality audiovisual system.

The author in 1986, outlining the year's goals at the Annual Management Policy Meeting held on January 10.

Above: A small group discussing quality problems.
Below: The author in March 1983 on the opening day of Katano Matsushita
Co., Ltd., a factory staffed by the physically handicapped.

Top: Employees reading the company creed at one of the daily morning meetings held throughout the Matsushita group.
Center: Lunching with employees in the company cafeteria.
Bottom: Participating in the tug-of-war at a company athletic meet.

Some of Matsushita's distributors in Europe: (*top*) Belgium; (*center*) the Netherlands; (*bottom*) Denmark.

Panasonic de Costa Rica
S.A.

NEICO Electric Industrial Co.
(Iran) Ltd.

Matsushita Electric Co. (East
Africa), Tanzania.

At the dedication of a new
building of the Precision
Technology Center, Tan-
zania, on November 6,
1986.

MB Video G.m.b.H. in Osterode Harz, West Germany.

The Overseas Training Center in Osaka.

Visiting National do Brazil Ltda, in September 1982.

With Lee Kuan Yew, prime minister of Singapore, on August 20, 1981.

With King Hussein of Jordan and his wife in September 1983.

The November 1981 donation of $1 million to the Harvard Business School was attended by the dean, Dr. John H. McArthur (*front left*), and Konosuke Matsushita (*front right*).

The author with W. Hasenclever, the secretary general of the Max-Planck-Gesellschaft, in May 1988, when DM1 million was donated to that institution.

The author with President Raymond Gates of Panasonic Company, on the twenty-fifth anniversary of that Stateside sales firm.

With H.R.H. the Duke of Edinburgh in November 1984.

With Indira Gandhi, prime minister of India, in February 1982.

With Ahmed Abdallah Abderemane, president of the Republic of the Comoros, in April 1987.

With H.R.H. King Carl XVI Gustaf of Sweden in March 1982.

With H.R.H. Princess Margriet Francisca of the Netherlands in November 1982.

With President Rodrigo Carazo of Costa Rica in June 1980.

With President U San Yu, president of Burma, and his wife in July 1983.

At National Peruana S.A. in Peru in 1955.

At a Go tournament of Kansai district executives in August 1985.

At Mt. Yushan, Taiwan's highest mountain, in 1984.

The author with his wife on a visit to the Leaning Tower of Pisa in August 1986.

and get co-workers to recognize, the value of someone who is plugging away at a task he dislikes. Fortified by that support, he will be better motivated in his next assignment, glad he stuck it out with the company.

A pleasant environment doesn't necessarily mean that everybody is a big happy family or the job is easy. On the contrary, there may be tough production quotas or seemingly impossible technological problems. Yet success is that much sweeter when it is hard-earned. My transfer to West Electric and that rough first year were tolerable because I knew my superiors appreciated my efforts. Otherwise, it would have been unbearable.

Feedback: The Staff of Management

The key components of a worthwhile career are interesting assignments, decent work conditions, and good bosses. Matsushita certainly offers the first two, so an employee who has good supervisors is thrice-blessed. But a talented person who is stuck with a lousy or incompetent superior can languish unnoticed and become bitter and discontented. It's too late to complain on retiring that, "If the boss had been a little more understanding, my career at Matsushita would have been more productive."

As division director, I occasionally met informally for frank discussions with groups of supervisors in the thirty to thirty-five age bracket. Usually there were five or six in a group; the most was about ten. I tried to be accessible and told the staff they could bring any problem or idea to me. Perhaps partly because they were young, they talked candidly about all kinds of issues. Whenever I visited an out-of-the-way Matsushita factory or smaller laboratory, I also set time aside to meet with the employees. Call it bottom-up management or keeping in touch with the grass roots, I listened to employees and tried to implement their ideas whenever feasible. At least they knew that somebody cared about what they were doing. That can make all the difference.

Employees in their twenties are still wet behind the ears and don't know what is going on, but men in their thirties and forties are more responsible and they know what they are talking about. Middle-level managers must be encouraged to speak up and be shown that their ideas are taken seriously.

When a brainstorming session or a one-on-one discussion led me to take some action, I tried to minimize any negative effects on the people I had talked to. If, for example, someone had to be transferred to remove a bottleneck, I made sure the source of that suggestion was protected. Loyalty to your subordinates is an iron rule for any supervisor.

An employee who complains may not realize what the real problem is: an effective supervisor has to be very perceptive to figure it out. Then you have to do something about it, not let the matter slide or hope it will go away. Subordinates respond appreciatively and feel, "I'll work my tail off for this guy." That was my reaction when I was young, and later in life I always told myself, "Be a good listener."

Another advantage of personnel transfers is that employees get to serve under a variety of people. Each new supervisor is a fresh start, an opportunity to win recognition. In laboratories, for example, there are many lone wolfs and highly skilled but temperamental professionals who lose interest in their work if there is a personality conflict with the supervisor. They can be rescued and recharged by a transfer when another research facility requests help with a new project. It depends on how you look at it, of course, but you also learn something about life and human nature by serving under a bastard.

Some of my personnel decisions apparently were regarded as bizarre. To cite an extreme example, when I was running the air conditioner division, I switched the chiefs of manufacturing and sales. I wanted to broaden them and I thought they both could handle an entirely different situation. The sales chief, who had regarded his counterpart as some kind of grease monkey utterly ignorant of how hard it was to sell his finished product, now had to deal with on-time delivery and tight specifications. The engineer discovered the world wasn't full of customers lined up to buy his machines. It was a very successful move; soon I had two paragons of cooperativeness working for me.

Some of my transfers as president, too, occasioned bitter objections. Once, without warning, I named a division director for personnel. "I've never done personnel work. It's not my line," he complained. Tired of this "no-experience" plea, I said, "Look at me. I was never president before. I wasn't prepared either." He couldn't say a word. In most cases, this line was an effective clincher.

A mid-level manager moving to a difficult or important job or who has been unexpectedly promoted over many other candidates must proceed cautiously. Trying to hit the ground running in a new position is a good way to fall on your face. No one, no matter how brilliant, can immediately size up a new situation; it takes about six months to get the lay of the land. Hasty action only triggers sardonic grimaces and snide comments. Meanwhile, the newcomer agonizes over the staff's unresponsiveness. Think of yourself as a relief pitcher coming in from the bullpen and be sure to warm up before throwing that first pitch.

Shift Competence, Not Misfits

Personnel transfers are not as easy as moving pieces on a chessboard. The first reassignments I made as president had no discernible impact. The division directors, who have complete responsibility for their bailiwick, were reluctant to part with competent people. To put teeth into the policy, I made it a rule that all transferees must have an A rating in the annual personnel review. This spread the fast-track people around and boosted overall productivity. I also made service in three divisions a prerequisite for promotion to manager.

The transfers pumped new blood through Matsushita's hardening arteries and kept the regular staff in each division on their toes. I'm not aware of any failures. If transfers are made for the good of the company, as opposed to such reasons as punishment or favoritism, they will work out well. Honda Motor's experience with personnel shifts is also instructive. The decisions are made by an executive director or higher, a person who is not running a plant. He has the best interests of the whole company in mind and can override departmental opposition. When Honda starts a new project, the best engineers and specialists are picked from throughout the company. If the departments were allowed to nominate candidates, they would send second- or third-rate people.

Sharing experience is another way to diffuse know-how. Everyone improvises solutions to problems that arise on the job. Sharing these ad hoc methods avoids every plant or division having to reinvent the wheel. Matsushita makes VCRs at factories in Okayama, Kadoma in Osaka, and Yamagata. When a quality control specialist in Okayama, for example, comes up with a new technique, he is sent to Yamagata to explain it. Not wanting to be outshone, the Yamagata staff are alert for improvements they in turn can share. These exchanges encourage a friendly, productive rivalry.

Innovation or reform always clashes with the status quo. Success stories, even very modest ones, help to overcome resistance. Just as a picture is worth a thousand words, an Okayama worker demonstrating a better test for defects is living proof that the technique works. Development assistance officials use a similar method to improve public health programs in the Third World. Instead of starting with lectures on personal hygiene—wash your hands before eating, be careful of raw foods—doctors treat patients with antibiotics. The quick, dramatic results give instant credibility to modern sanitation and medical techniques.

Introducing new know-how is an implicit criticism of how things have been done, so some workers usually oppose the change and others are indifferent. Demonstrating the technique convinces most employees, and the recalcitrants go along. Management must keep the workplace open to innovation.

Another way we do that at Matsushita Electric is by a strong employee suggestion program. In recent years, employees have submitted about 6.5 million ideas annually. People actually doing a task are in the best position to improve the process; the program taps this priceless reservoir of hands-on experience.

A suggestion program depends on management being open and receptive to new ideas. If supervisors just pay lip service to the program, then employees don't get any feedback and they lose enthusiasm. This wellspring of creativity can be poisoned by neglect.

At Matsushita, every six months a screening committee reviews all suggestions. The committee's job isn't to shoot down ideas; they try to adopt as many as possible. Cash prizes are awarded based on the value of the concept. Quality control groups have received more than ¥1 million for a notion. Over the last few years there has been a qualitative improvement in suggestions, apparently due to accelerated technological change and a better-trained work force, and we receive some brilliant, original schemes.

Women at Matsushita

In recent years, Japanese corporations have begun to utilize female personnel more effectively. No longer are young women restricted to pouring tea or dead-end assembly line or secretarial positions. A milestone toward equality was the Equal Employment Opportunity Law passed in 1985 (effective

April 1986), which banned discrimination against women in hiring, assignments, and promotion. Women are now a highly visible, important part of the Matsushita work force, a welcome change from the past.

In 1984, Matsushita had a booth at a Moscow trade fair. Unlike such shows elsewhere, exhibitors cannot hire local staff in the Soviet Union but must bring Russian-speaking personnel to look after the booth. We found an employee fluent in Russian, Ms. Suzuki (not her real name), working in Matsushita's Museum of Technology in Osaka, where she explained high-technology products to visitors.

Ms. Suzuki was a hit in Moscow, demonstrating the latest electrical products and answering questions in Russian. Changing into a kimono, she doubled as a hostess at a Matsushita reception for high Soviet trade officials. Ms. Suzuki delighted the guests by playing *"Katchusha"* and *"Sakura, Sakura"* on the electronic organ. No male employee had that combination of linguistic, musical, and social skills. Many female employees have lived or been educated abroad and become fluent in foreign languages. They put the men to shame in the company's annual foreign-language speech contests.

Matsushita's appliance divisions offer women many opportunities to capitalize on their experience as homemakers. Women designed a new washing machine rotor. Two female engineers developed an automatic bread-making machine called the "Home Bakery," of which a million units were sold in 1987. Women at Matsushita are working as software engineers, architects designing system kitchens, and consumer advisors. They are also helping to promote an unusual import for a consumer electronics company—Famous Grouse and Highland Park Scotch—by holding tasting sessions at department stores and liquor stores. There was opposition to a Matsushita company handling a product like Scotch whisky, but it faded away, and we now have an efficient marketing team and sales have risen steadily.

I am delighted at the increase in the number of women in management—in 1987 there were about forty—at Matsushita, a trend that will continue. As a sign of the times, the more outspoken now complain to the personnel department about suspected sexist discrimination.

Building Corporate Solidarity

At Matsushita there is top to bottom support for company policy, a unity of purpose often made fun of by critics who say, "All Matsushita employees think and talk alike," but conformity to company policy doesn't mean employees are stripped of their individuality. In other words, there is no contradiction between a common purpose and solidarity as an enterprise, on the one hand, and distinctive personalities as individual employees, on the other.

When I first joined Matsushita I thought there was excessive emphasis on company philosophy, but in recent years I have changed my mind. A company like Matsushita, unified by a coherent outlook and shared goals, is a wonderful anomaly in Japan today.

Solidarity is an important tradition. The New Year's Annual Management Policy Meeting, for example, is held every January 10, even if the date falls on a Sunday. About seven thousand Matsushita supervisory personnel gather to hear it. This assemblage itself is a tribute to organizational ardor. Other companies admit they couldn't hold such a function. Their employees, pleading personal reasons or pressing duties, wouldn't show up. At Matsushita, the January meeting is a custom that takes precedence over other work.

Similar clothing in the workplace, a uniform if you will, helps to create teamwork. In recent years, thousands of foreign researchers and business executives have come to Japan to study Japanese-style management, and many have worked in factories to get hands-on experience. Among them was a student from a famous French university who trained at a Japanese electrical equipment maker for six months. He came from a well-to-do family and was assured of a good position upon his return to France. Because of this elitist background, he was dismayed at his dormitory accommodations: a small tatami room with the washroom and toilet down the hall. When he started, he was given a pair of blue overalls and told, "Wear these to work tomorrow." His dignity was further affronted when he learned they were the same kind that factory workers wore.

The French trainee was mollified the next morning to see that all supervisors—foremen, section chiefs, and even the plant manager—wore the same blue overalls. Gradually he grew accustomed to his "uniform." By the end of six months, he had been converted to Japanese-style egalitarianism and said he would recommend the practice in France. A typical feature of Japanese workplaces, uniforms help to create solidarity.

U.S. supervisory personnel don't wear uniforms and they usually have their own offices and secretaries. In Japan, a personal office is a perk reserved for company directors and above. Below that level, most companies use large, open offices with employees and supervisors working side by side and across from each other. (In Honda Motor Company, even directors work in large offices with other personnel, but that is an exception.)

IBM is a U.S. company that values uniformity. At any IBM office worldwide the staff wear white shirts. Several years ago I visited the IBM headquarters in New York. By that time even some Matsushita employees wore colored shirts at work, so I was very surprised that every IBM male worker had a white shirt and a short haircut. There was an impressive sense of order.

New employees in Japan are instructed in bowing and proper etiquette—how to present and accept a name card, make an introduction, pour tea for visitors, and so on. These are important aspects of business behavior throughout the world and should be taken seriously. Such matters of form indicate attitude. Etiquette should also be heart-felt lest conventional gestures betray insincerity or disrespect. Employees who learn the forms and follow them all the time—for example, by bowing at precisely the correct angle—will internalize deference and politeness.

To be honest, when I joined Matsushita in 1937, I hated the daily ritual of morning assemblies—everyone reciting the company creed and pledge, and singing the company song. I suspect many of our young employees today feel the same way. But by daily repetition of these laudable ideas about service, honesty, and teamwork, you gradually take them to heart. At these assemblies, somebody in each group or section makes a short presentation on a topic of his or her choice. Speakers may discuss a book they have read, a conversation they had with a friend the day before, or a thought that occurred to them on the job. Each person speaks once or twice a month, depending on the unit's size. The objective is to train employees to express their thoughts through informal public speaking. Even personnel who pay no attention when the factory manager makes an announcement listen carefully to peer presentations because they know their turn is coming. The system works.

Mr. Matsushita is invariably courteous regardless of the other person's rank or status. At testimonial parties for retailers, for example, he used to bow politely even to junior store clerks and pour them a cup of saké. He lowered his head in a special way when bowing, fairly deep but not exaggerated. I often stood beside him on such occasions, but I could never bow quite the same way. Either I didn't bend far enough or it was too deep and seemed affected. My bow was just a neck-stretching exercise; Mr. Matsushita's expressed his unassuming personality.

Contributing to Society

I mentioned earlier that the philosophy at Matsushita is "The mission of an enterprise is to contribute to society." This dates from 1932, when Mr. Matsushita was deeply influenced by religion. He realized that "To succeed in business requires more than just hard work. I must always be aware of my responsibility to society." Mr. Matsushita identified with this philosophy and it became the core of his management principles. These values, sometimes called the "Panasonic Way," have been taught to all employees ever since.

This management philosophy ultimately means that the individual employee is recognized as a valuable part of the enterprise. Each person must believe, "I am doing worthwhile work that benefits the community." Otherwise, the principles would be mere slogans. This personal commitment turns abstract values into concrete accomplishments.

In Europe, work is regarded as hard and unpleasant, and vacations are a respite from toil. But as long as work is viewed as an obligation, annual leave—even if it consists of two or three weeks on a tropical isle—will never compensate for the rest of the year. But when work is seen as an opportunity to serve the public, the employee feels ennobled.

In September 1977, a Japan Air Lines jet en route from Paris to Tokyo was hijacked by the radical Japanese Red Army to Dhaka in Bangladesh. Negotiations with the hijackers took four days. A passenger later reported that the one bright spot in the ordeal was the JAL flight attendants' bravery, as they cheerfully tended the passengers and sustained morale throughout the long confinement. When the captors finally announced that the hostages would be freed, one attendant said to the purser, "We may be kept on board even after the passengers are let go." There was no panic or self-pity in the statement; she was a professional coolly assessing the situation. Dedication gave these young women extraordinary mental and physical strength.

Management principles and corporate policy hinge on whether individual employees have this sense of mission. Managers can't impose commitment. It comes from everyone doing his or her best.

When I became president, a reporter asked me, "What kind of company do you want Matsushita to be?" I replied, "A place where employees genuinely look forward to coming to work."

Two companies in the same industry can be as unlike as night and day. In Company A, the employees dislike the job, the boss, and the corporation. In Company B, they are loyal and give one hundred percent to the company. The difference often is in whether the supervisors care about the people under them and appreciate their difficulties, frustrations, and contributions.

Some operations, such as manufacturing and sales, directly affect a company's success and are statistically quantifiable. Production quotas are met and sales curves go up. Although employees suffer a certain amount of stress from being under top management's scrutiny, they also have the satisfaction of concrete accomplishments. However, warehouse operations and public relations play a supporting role; their contribution is intangible or difficult to measure. Nevertheless, the man at the top has to remember these unsung heroes, too.

Working Toward Goals

I am often asked to speak at wedding receptions, and one of my favorite themes is goals. I tell the newlyweds that the couple without a dream is sad, but the couple that only builds castles in the air is helpless. A marriage where partners share aspirations and strive together to accomplish them is blessed by the gods.

Happiness is the undaunted pursuit of personal objectives. Even as we attain one goal we set a new one. Goals thirty or forty years ahead are no good. You don't know what to do today or tomorrow to reach them. Two or three objectives to be attained in six months is about right. The specific goal is not very important as long as it is personal. If the objectives also involve the family and community, all the better.

Let me illustrate my point with the tale of two laborers. A minister walking through a European town noticed a hod carrier with a load of bricks. The man wore a disgruntled look and moved slowly. "What are you doing?" the minister asked. "Just what it looks like. I'm hauling bricks," the man replied. A while later, the minister spotted another hod carrier. This man walked briskly and was singing a song. "What are you doing?" the minister asked him. "I'm building a magnificent cathedral," he responded. One man begrudged his labor and diminished himself. The other dreamed of spires piercing the sky and linked himself to the Creator.

An acquaintance of mine grew up in a rural family and hated farm life. As soon as he could, he moved to the city and found a job. Now, he spends weekends and holidays working in his vegetable garden, a small rented plot in the suburbs. Again, work done under duress is agony, but the same activity can be delightful if we want to do it. As Gorky and Confucius said, work you enjoy is the greatest pleasure in life. After all, it is the dominant activity of our lives.

Every time a new marathon record is set it reminds me that human potential is unlimited. The marathon has been an official event since the start of the modern games in Athens in 1896. The record time established that year was two hours fifty-eight minutes and fifty seconds. The world record set by Carlos Lopes of Portugal in the Amsterdam Marathon in 1985 was two hours seven minutes and twelve seconds. In eighty-nine years the time had been shortened by fifty-one minutes thirty-eight seconds.

Running styles and training methods have improved enormously and athletes are much stronger now. Yet the basic reason for the faster times is the runners' relentless determination to break their own records.

Many athletes have broken barriers once thought to be the limit of human achievement. Champions have accomplished "impossible" feats by setting brutal training regimens and following them day after day, month after month. Amateurs and world-class distance runners share this dedication. Sweat-suit clad runners silently running along the street, determined to break their own best time, are a familiar sight in Japan. There is virtually no limit to human performance. That applies to business, as well.

In Totsuka, a small town ten minutes by train from Yokohama, there is a National-brand appliance store run by a couple whom I shall call the Satos. In 1972, a large supermarket opened across the street from their store; the appliance section was ten to twenty times larger than the Satos' shop, and the prices were lower. In these circumstances, the average small retailer would have bowed to the inevitable and quit.

Sato was distraught for a while but instead of giving up, he began looking for a competitive edge. He visited supermarkets in the Tokyo area, studied their appliance sections and found a window of opportunity. At supermarkets, delivery of major appliances took two or three days, and service calls took a day or two. Most clerks were impersonal at best to customers, and many couldn't explain the stock.

Sato began a two-hour delivery service for appliances. He made immediate service calls, not only for National products but for all brands. As a result of this super service, Sato developed closer ties with customers than he had ever had before. And he became confident of survival.

The Sato family grew closer together during the crisis. Mrs. Sato, who had previously only waited on customers when her husband was out on a service call, became a full partner in the business, knowledgeable about the products and keeping the books. Their teen-age daughter worked in the shop after school and on weekends. When business picked up, they doubled the floor space to make the cramped display area more attractive. The Satos now have two branch stores.

"I'm grateful to the supermarket," says Mr. Sato. "Otherwise, my wife and I would have puttered along in the old way. But when Goliath arrived, I learned how to run a business. Our family became a close-knit team. To my delight, my son has agreed to take over the stores when I retire."

The Satos fought overwhelming odds and won. They stayed the course and pulled off a gold-medal performance.

5
Operating in the World Economy

As I mentioned in Chapter 3, the long-term strategy I adopted called for 25 percent from production offshore, 25 percent to be exported, and 50 percent for the domestic market. In 1977, we were exporting about 30 percent, and overseas production was only about 14 percent.

Signs of a protectionist backlash against the flood of Japanese exports made it necessary for us to increase the role of our foreign subsidiaries. The yen was stable at about ¥220 to the dollar, and it was inconceivable that Japan's trading partners would stand idly by while Japanese goods captured their markets. Matsushita Electric should aim to balance export sales with production abroad, I thought.

A few executives objected on the grounds that decreased production at home would make some personnel redundant. But I convinced them that the day of export offensives was over, and we had to bite the bullet.

At Matsushita Electric, six principles govern overseas investment. These sometimes have to be applied flexibly because conditions vary from country to country, but experience has shown that straying too far from them invites trouble. The principles are: (1) Matsushita Electric's activities must be welcomed in the host country; (2) business activities must be carried out in accordance with the policies of the government of the host country; we should strive to make it understand our objectives and methods; (3) we must transfer technology; (4) our overseas manufacturing companies must make products that are internationally competitive in quality, performance, and cost; (5) profitability must be built into the corporate structure of our overseas companies, so that they are able to generate the funds necessary to expand their activities; and (6) the venture should train workers in the host country.

In the final analysis, local approval is the *sine qua non* of success. The employees must feel that the venture is compatible with their nation's interests. Without that good will, the subsidiary will neither benefit the host country nor earn a profit for us.

Success hinges upon the work force. At Matsushita Electric we have long had a saying: "Good employees make good products." By "good," we mean well trained and motivated, and this holds equally true for foreign operations.

In this respect, I take off my hat to Honda Motor, whose overseas plants are always impressive. I toured a motorcycle factory in Nigeria, for example, and found to my surprise that quality and productivity were virtually the same as at a Honda plant in Japan. Given the disparity in education between Japanese and Nigerian workers, there had been some question whether local employees could handle certain technologically sophisticated operations. But the Japanese manager had trained them to his own high standards.

Honda wisely staffs foreign plants with top-quality executives. You might expect to find outstanding managers at their flagship operation in Ohio, but few Japanese companies can match the caliber of personnel they send to the Third World.

Hearing the plant manager in Nigeria give employees directions in Japanese, I asked him, "Can they speak Japanese?" He laughed and said, "No, but they understand what I mean. When somebody does a good job, I praise him. If an employee fouls up, I chew him out. That's all you have to do. I don't give detailed instructions."

Rather than express himself awkwardly in Hausa or Ibo, the manager preferred to use Japanese because he could convey an emotional dimension—admiration and respect when lauding an accomplishment or a no-nonsense tone when correcting an error. It almost seemed as if Soichiro Honda, the founder and engineering genius of the auto giant, were speaking. In fact, his disciples have now spread all over the world.

As I was leaving, the manager said jokingly, "Tell them at my head office that another company's president has visited here, but we have never seen the top man from Honda." A plant manager in the Soichiro Honda mold doesn't need head-quarters' supervision. The man in Nigeria was the confident, can-do type, capable of handling anything.

I also visited the Honda plant in Manaus, Brazil, and found it equally efficient and run by the same kind of dynamic manager. The automaker can transplant its philosophy and pro-duction system anywhere. The Honda experience shows that the Japanese approach to diligence—a tough, serious attitude to work—and organizational dynamism can be used abroad.

Overseas subsidiaries will eventually be operated by local personnel. During the transition phase, they should be thor-oughly grounded in the best aspects of Japanese-style manage-ment.

The Japanese Touch

Professor Richard T. Pascale of Stanford University's Graduate School of Business and the coauthor, with Anthony G. Athos, of *The Art of Japanese Management*, uses the case-study method and role playing in his classes. In one scenario, Com-pany A is about to launch a new product—let's say it's a hair dryer—when they learn that Company B will soon release a bet-ter one. Company A has to suspend the launch and refashion its model. The problem is for A's product development (PD) chief to obtain the agreement of the manufacturing division (MD) chief to start all over again. Professor Pascale plays the head of manufacturing and students take turns as product development chief.

In one classroom exercise, the first student said that Company B was putting out a product that would obviously outsell theirs, and he wanted the manufacturing division to make an improved version. The MD chief (Pascale) replied that he was just making what PD had requested; a decision to stop production or redesign the product was entirely up to the PD manager.

The student's approach failed to persuade the MD head, and two more also tried unsuccessfully. The fourth role player, a Japanese, had listened to the give-and-take and tried a different tack. First he praised the manufacturing division for turning the PD's concept into a fine commercial product. He went on to say that they had just discovered that Company B was coming out with an even better dryer. He asked the MD chief's opinion: Under the new circumstances, would their version sell? He quickly added that he personally thought Company B's dryer would preempt the market. Since PD had initiated the product, it was responsible and would do everything in its power to correct the situation. He concluded by asking for MD's recommendation.

Won over by this conciliatory approach, the MD chief replied that in its present form their hair dryer wouldn't sell, so the company would have to improve it. MD would start work immediately and requested PD's full cooperation.

Exporting the Matsushita Spirit

The key to success in overseas subsidiaries is instilling Matsushita methods and attitudes in local personnel. More than five thousand foreign employees have been trained at our

Overseas Training Institute in Osaka. In the early years the curriculum was heavily weighted toward technology; the emphasis now is on management techniques. We also have training facilities in Indonesia, Singapore, Brazil, Tanzania, and the United States.

Our experience with a subsidiary in Costa Rica, Panasonic de Costa Rica S.A., is an example of what can go right and wrong with offshore production. People made the difference.

Costa Ricans are genial by nature, and in 1966, when we established this company to produce dry batteries and radios, the country was politically stable. But in late 1982 the senior person in our eight-man Japanese staff was killed by guerrillas. We immediately evacuated all dependents to neighboring Panama and instructed the staff to leave as soon as possible. At that point, I received a personal letter from the president of Costa Rica, Luis Alberto Monge, apologizing for the incident and appealing to me not to close the factory. Costa Rica lacks industry, he said, and this company was a particularly valuable asset because its exports earned foreign exchange. Although I sympathized with President Monge, we couldn't jeopardize our employees' lives.

As an ad hoc solution, we moved all Japanese staff to Miami and resumed production under a sort of "remote-controlled" management. Each morning the Costa Rican supervisor telephoned a status report to Miami. Machinery in need of repair was dismantled and brought to Florida on Saturdays. The next day, our technicians showed the Costa Rican mechanics how to fix it, and then they took the equipment back to the plant on Monday.

Initially, we were uncertain whether the Costa Ricans could run the factory without any Japanese on the scene, but they worked like Trojans to keep it functioning, knowing how important it was to their country and to Matsushita Electric. Thanks to employee unity and dedication, in a year's time it was more efficient than when our people were there.

Iran: The Panasonic Way Meets the Islamic Revolution

We had a similar experience in Iran, which I visited a few months before the Islamic revolution. The key person there was M. F. Ghassemi, president of NEICO Electric Industrial Co. (Iran), Ltd., whom I first met in Teheran on August 1, 1978, on my return from climbing Mt. Damavand. He had been the sole agent for Matsushita Electric products and later started manufacturing radios and TVs. We provided him with technical assistance, which led to the formation of a joint venture. The NEICO plant is in the suburbs of Isfahan, an ancient capital established by Shah Abbas I in 1598.

Ghassemi is 5 feet 11 inches tall, stocky and dark-complexioned, with classical Iranian features. He's a shrewd, energetic businessman and a very tough bargainer. In Osaka, his visits to Japan are known as the "Ghassemi typhoon." But that August night he was subdued, even sad. I thought perhaps he was ill, but it may just have been the realization that awesome political changes were in the wind.

Shortly after I left Iran, the Abadan theater was burned down with great loss of life. In September 1978, Shah Mohammad Reza Pahlavi declared martial law, but a general strike on October 16 cut off water, electricity, and other public services. Fighting broke out between Shiite Moslem forces, inspired by the Ayatollah Ruhollah Khomeini, and military units loyal to the shah. In January 1979, the shah left Iran, and politicians, generals, and businessmen closely identified with the monarchy also began to flee the country.

Concerned about the safety of our nine employees who were in Iran with the joint venture, we recalled their dependents and directed all Japanese staff to leave expeditiously. In February 1979, the government was toppled and on April 1 the Ayatollah Khomeini proclaimed the Islamic Republic of Iran. About 10,000 supporters of the monarchy were executed.

Despite the chaos and bloodshed, Ghassemi never wavered. He told a Japanese colleague, "I'm Iranian. I started with nothing and built up this company. Even if I were to lose everything, if all my assets were confiscated by the revolutionary government, I would have no regrets. After all, these things belong to the fatherland. So I'm not afraid." Sometimes a life-or-death situation can reveal surprising aspects of a person. With his wealth and influence, Ghassemi could have shifted his assets abroad and left Iran, as many industrialists were doing. But under that gruff businessman's exterior, he had strong nationalistic feelings.

The Japanese vice president of the joint venture was so impressed by Ghassemi's courage that he volunteered to stay in Iran. As Ghassemi was relatively inexperienced at running a plant, our man thought that without a senior Japanese engineer on the scene, the Iranians might not be able to keep it going.

By this time, of course, the Iran–Iraq war was underway. The Islamic Revolutionary Council had banned alcohol, food was in short supply, and Iraqi air raids were a constant threat. TV afforded no relief to a Japanese, since it relayed programs about the Koran from morning to night. Our engineer's willingness to share the hardship and danger inspired the Iranian employees, who wanted to show him they were competent to run the operation. F. Haddadi, the plant manager, subtly declaring independence, told him, "If you have to leave, we can keep the factory running, I promise."

Many joint ventures or foreign-owned subsidiaries in Iran have been nationalized, but this company is still in private hands. Ghassemi's extraordinary character pulled the employees together despite the political and economic turmoil.

Ghassemi came to the company's tenth anniversary celebration at the Royal Hotel in Osaka on March 29, 1984. In my remarks, I said, "This company has weathered political upheaval and war to become one of Iran's top corporations.

We are all indebted to Mr. Ghassemi for his brave, resourceful leadership."

Technical Training in Tanzania

In 1966, we established Matsushita Electric Co. (East Africa) (MEFCA) in the United Republic of Tanzania. The nation was formed two years earlier by the union of Tanganyika and the two islands of Zanzibar and Pemba. Mt. Kilimanjaro, Africa's highest peak, towers above the border between Tanzania and Kenya. Dar es Salaam, the capital and major seaport, was once a shipping point for the slave trade.

MEFCA, set up at the request of the Tanzanian government, makes dry cell batteries and radios. Tanzania is a socialist country, and some people at Matsushita Electric had misgivings about investing there, but hard work and dedication have paid off handsomely. Some things that are taken for granted in Japan—employees starting work on time and staying the whole day—are not automatically part of the picture there.

We provide breakfast for Tanzanian employees, replicating a successful experiment in Indonesia where the workers were poor and so usually came to work without having eaten breakfast. By mid-morning output slipped, and many workers, made careless by lack of nourishment and fatigue, were injured. Serving breakfast insured that employees got a morning meal. Absenteeism and injuries declined, and punctuality and overall efficiency rose. Although the practice seems paternalistic, it was a practical response to a serious problem. The company also has a vegetable farm nearby to keep the cafeteria well supplied.

In 1984, we established the Precision Technology Center near the factory, providing the tools, materials, and two instructors. Under the original agreement, Matsushita Electric was to operate the center for three years and then turn it over to the government. I was invited to Tanzania in November

1986 for the transfer, and also to attend both a graduation ceremony and the dedication of a new administration building. After my arrival I learned that the government wished to defer the transfer, and we agreed to operate it for another two years.

The center admits twenty students annually and offers a two-year course in the electrical engineering and mechanical trades. The latter includes instruction in using metal presses, jigs, and tools, and in die-making. Upon graduation, trainees were supposed to return to their parent company, but as so many were recruited by other firms anxious to acquire skilled workers, graduates today receive their diplomas only after they have been back at their original company for a year. The first two directors of the center were Japanese; in autumn 1986, a Tanzanian was appointed.

Located at Mikocheni, along Bagamoyo Road to the north of Dar es Salaam, the center's six buildings are laid out on spacious grounds. The staff started with one building and gradually added the others. The facilities are an impressive symbol of Tanzania's commitment to industrialization.

Transferring Japanese-style Management

By November, the Tanzanian rainy season is over and it is the start of summer. I hadn't been to Dar es Salaam in seven years, but before leaving Japan I was told the temperature there was about 86°F (30°C). Nevertheless, because of the graduation ceremony, I wore a dark blue suit and a necktie. Inside buildings or in the shade the temperature was in the middle eighties, but in the sun it was over 100°F! Dripping wet and constantly wiping away the perspiration, I realized I was the only person in a suit. Everyone else, including the Japanese staff, looked cool and comfortable in their safari-style clothes.

First we dedicated the new administration building. The minister of education, the vice minister of construction, and I were to cut the tape. The entranceway has a porchlike front with two pillars that support an overhanging roof, and the tape was stretched between the pillars. In Japan, a broad ribbon is used on such occasions. Stepping up to the entrance, I thought, "That's a very thin tape," and discovered that it was a vinyl electric cord made of intertwined red and white strands. A woman held out a tray with a pair of wire cutters. I thought, "Well, this is a vocational institute and the students cut this kind of wire, so they must have chosen it intentionally."

Actually, the Tanzanians had wanted to have a Japanese-style opening with ribbon and scissors, but the ribbon was not delivered on time, and the cord was a last-minute substitution. "It looks like a ribbon," I thought and started to cut. No luck. I couldn't sever the damn thing. Looking to my left, I saw that both Tanzanian officials had deftly cut it. Only the representative of high-tech Japan, an engineer by training and ex-president of Matsushita Electric to boot, stood there sweating profusely in his dark business suit, unable to get through that cord.

Fortunately, I didn't have to display manual dexterity at the graduation ceremony, which was held in a classroom and attended by about 120 people, including the trainees, government officials, and executives from the sponsoring companies. K. Maganya, the first Tanzanian director, ran the proceedings. He turned to me and the other guests and bowed deeply, and each graduate also bowed as he received his diploma. It must be a Tanzanian custom, I thought, but I was wrong. The government had told our staff to teach not just vocational skills but also the Japanese work style, so the curriculum included Japanese attitudes and etiquette. The students' dignified bows were worthy of a graduation ceremony in Osaka or Tokyo. In my brief remarks I said, "Matsushita management is essentially personnel development, which ultimately means self-reliance, training a person to stand on his own two feet. I hope that you will accept any challenge that comes along."

At the party afterwards, Maganya proposed a toast in

Japanese: "Despite my inadequate qualifications, I have been appointed director of this center. . . ." He had written the text out in Roman letters beforehand and memorized the polite, self-effacing Japanese phrases. Then, with great panache, Maganya raised his right hand and said *"Kampai!"* But there was no glass in it. It's not the custom at a Tanzanian party or reception to wait until the host proposes a toast. An event begins with the first arrivals, who just start eating and drinking. Worried that the party might begin before he could make a proper toast, the flustered Maganya had forgotten to fill a glass for himself. He did it over again, this time with a drink in his hand, and carried it off perfectly.

Eight Matsushita Electric personnel have taught at the center, and two have headed it. The second director accompanied me on this trip and told me some of his experiences. He tried to encourage Tanzanians to be curious, think for themselves, and solve problems by asking the instructor or reading books. Their basic skill level is low, he said, and there is still a strong sense (a legacy of colonialism) that faithfully following instructions—doing what you are told—is sufficient. Equating personal improvement with service to Tanzania, he urged the students to upgrade their ability as a form of patriotism.

There are several technical institutes supported by foreign aid funds in Tanzania. Generally, the instructors cover an intensive curriculum regardless of whether the students are interested or really learning the subjects. Often the frustrated teachers complete assignments or projects for the students. The record shows that the students have had, for example, forty hours of instruction in metal working; in fact, they can't operate a lathe.

"If this center is a success," the former director said, "it's because we geared the curriculum to the trainee's level and patiently allowed them to practice and try until they could do it."

The center has Matsushita-style morning assemblies where students make short presentations. At first their remarks were all complaints, such as "The cafeteria food is lousy," or "Portions are too small." Gradually, their attitudes changed, and now they talk about personal goals and the importance of their training to Tanzania. In Japan or East Africa, the major objective of education is to inculcate initiative and follow-through.

An oft-used word in Swahili, the official language of Tanzania, is *polepole*, which means "slowly" or "a little bit at a time." Sometimes it seems as if everything in Tanzania is done *polepole* and schedules are for reference only. The Japanese, who are always on the go and hate to waste time, have to gear down to a slower speed. Life moves to a gentler rhythm, and our teachers had to make a cultural adjustment.

Tanzania is a poor country with few natural resources, the principal export being sisal. The economy is underdeveloped, partly because of long colonial domination by Germany and Great Britain, when it was known as Tanganyika. Since winning independence in 1961, the government has been chronically short of foreign exchange and drought has badly hurt agriculture.

At the graduation party, I was told that the greatest delicacy in Tanzania is lobster, but it is expensive and rarely available. Next in order of preference are chicken, pork, and beef. Beef is ranked low because the cattle are thin—feed is in short supply—and the meat is not very tasty. Roads and public transportation are poor. The technical center, for example, is rather far from Dar es Salaam, but the trainees walk to and from classes each day. Shank's mare is the primary way of getting around Tanzania. Everywhere you see people walking.

A visitor from Osaka is struck by the contrast between affluent, bustling Japan and poor, slow-paced Tanzania. In which country are people happier? I'm not sure.

Cooperating with the Germans

Many pundits tell disaster stories of how Japanese management methods, rooted in groupism and consensus, have failed in the individualistic West. Granted, there is a profound difference in social norms, but it's not an insurmountable barrier.

In December 1982, Matsushita Electric and the West German automotive parts manufacturer Robert Bosch G.m.b.H. established a joint venture, MB Video G.m.b.H., in West Germany to make VCRs. About fifteen German employees were brought to Japan for training. We were worried that dissimilarities in national character would impede factory operations. The Germans are rationalistic and want clear-cut job descriptions and work rules, whereas the Japanese stress cooperation, solidarity, and team spirit. Furthermore, the German group included women and some married workers. Could they be taught the Panasonic Way in one month? The fears proved groundless, however. All the trainees were open and receptive to Japanese methods.

Later, J. Reinhart, who was slated to become the senior German executive in the joint venture, was sent to Japan for management training. Initially distraught at the assignment, Reinhart apparently thought involvement with "backward" Japan was a career dead end. But a few years later he had become an enthusiastic convert. In May 1986, Hans L. Merkle, chairman of Bosch, told me that the German employees for the joint venture were carefully selected. Bosch picked open-minded people who were unprejudiced against Japan or Japanese methods, and Reinhart met those criteria. Long interested in Japan, Merkle has given the fledgling company extraordinary support, and I really admire him.

At MB Video, Reinhart told me that during his training in Osaka he saw how workers cooperated on the assembly line and in other operations. If one person fell behind, others helped him or her. This hadn't been done at Bosch, Reinhart said. On his return, he had introduced the team concept and was very proud of the results. Now president of MB Video, Reinhart is no longer worried that association with Matsushita

Electric will prove fatal to his career. We have also benefited from this joint venture, for the technological exchange has helped both sides.

I visited the factory early one day and found that the Germans held morning assemblies, too. My personal feeling was that they didn't have to duplicate everything we do, but the meetings had become an integral part of plant life.

We had incorrectly formed the opinion that the Germans flatly refuse to work overtime. It's true that they will not stay late on short notice. If you ask them at three in the afternoon to work that night, the answer is usually no. German families do things together, and a worker who has promised his wife and children an outing won't disappoint them just because the foreman has a rush order. If you give German employees a week's advance notice, however, they will stay late.

Recently, some Matsushita Electric employees in Japan have been refusing to work overtime. Asked why by supervisors, they say, "My wife also works and today it's my turn to fix dinner. I've got to get home early and prepare things." I can imagine what the reaction would have been if I had said that to my boss forty years ago!

At MB Video I noticed that German workers have unusual manual dexterity and seem ambidextrous. Perhaps this is because from childhood they use a knife and fork. The Japanese are supposed to be quick with their hands, but actually we're only good with our right hand, the one we hold our chopsticks in. German workers have a natural advantage over their Japanese counterparts.

Private Sector Economic Cooperation Works

Setting up factories in the Third World is a form of economic aid that is really the job of the Japanese government, not the private sector. It's the function of the Japan International Cooperation Agency (JICA) and Official Development Assistance (ODA) programs. Corporations are private enterprises that have to pay attention to expenditures. Nevertheless, if management can spare the resources, private companies are many times more efficient at this task. They can move quickly and flexibly, and the individuals involved feel responsible for results. Sometimes the staff get so involved in a project that they become passionate advocates of local interests.

When problems arose at our factory in Tanzania, a Japanese employee returned to Osaka to report. His advice agreed one hundred percent with the Tanzanian government position; in fact, he sounded like one of their officials. Another time, our senior executive in Iran became ill and we suggested he return to Japan for treatment. "I'll come back, but please send someone to take my place," he said. The Iran–Iraq war was in full swing; we told him no suitable person was available. "I'll find one," he replied. He returned to Osaka and a short while later brought in a would-be replacement. I told the candidate, "We don't think it's absolutely necessary to send someone. We're not forcing you to go. There's a war on out there. You're sure you want to go?" "Yes," he said. "I know about the Iraqi air raids. But a Matsushita man should be there."

"I suppose you've discussed this with your wife and she has agreed to stay here while you go off. If something happens to you, she shouldn't blame the company," I said. In the end he went to Iran.

If this had been a government aid project in a war-torn country, the official on the scene would have said, "My three-year tour of duty here is up and I want to go back to Tokyo." Even if the individual was willing to stay longer, bureaucratic red tape probably would have made it impossible.

Another shortcoming of ODA is that Japan complies with the host country's wish list rather than providing the appropriate level of aid or technology. Developing countries usually want the most advanced machinery, which they often can't absorb or utilize.

An aid official told me that a certain country had requested fishing technology and Japan sent power-driven nets. During the two years that a Japanese technical team was there, the fish catch rose dramatically, to the delight of the local fishing industry, but later the motors broke down and nobody could repair them. It might have been better from the outset, the official said, to have sent several elderly Japanese fishermen to teach the art of mending fishing nets. Then the local people would have acquired practical know-how of lasting value.

In those Matsushita Electric overseas projects with an aid dimension, our principal goal is providing jobs. An automated factory in a country with a 40 percent unemployment rate is no godsend. In 1985, the Communist party candidate for mayor in Lima, Peru, won on a simple platform: one million breakfasts daily and drinking water for the city's slums. The Third World doesn't need high-tech plants equipped with industrial robots.

When Nigeria was flush with petrodollars, the government launched several ambitious industrialization products, including an automobile factory. But there was no technical infrastructure of mechanics and repair shops. Cars that were slightly damaged or broke down from normal use were scrapped! The record of failed development strategies proves that aid projects must have modest, attainable goals and be sustainable.

Hands-on Management

As president of Matsushita Electric, I missed the direct hands-on challenge of dealing with production or sales problems. When I headed the air conditioner division, I frequently strolled around the factory and visited retail outlets. Listening to division and section reports enabled me to spot promising younger employees and keep my finger on the corporate pulse. My successor as president, Akio Tanii, talks of "front-line-first management," keeping in close touch with on-site manufacturing and sales activities and not letting yourself become cloistered with the accountants at the head office. There's a world of difference between reading a report about a stalled product and talking to the grease-stained, frustrated engineers at a workbench. As Mr. Matsushita likes to say, "The only way to understand the flavor of salt is to put some on your tongue."

Once I became CEO it was virtually impossible to drop in at a factory and talk to engineers and production people informally. But I did regularly visit our overseas operations. There is no substitute for first-hand experience.

I mentioned that the smaller the unit, the better it is run. My pet theory to explain this is that headquarters' support is minimal for divisions with relatively small sales figures. The employees stay on top of their jobs; they don't count on the head office doing things for them. Independence fosters initiative. In this way, overseas subsidiaries have to look out for themselves. The staff in Malaysia, Iran, or Secaucus, New Jersey, can't send detailed memos on everything to us in Osaka. Because of time differences, the telephone isn't very effective: either the people out in the field or those at headquarters are usually half asleep. The person on the spot has to make the agonizing decisions. Personal responsibility and decentralized decision making strengthens the company and separates the real managers from the boys. Personnel who have served abroad come back more knowledgeable and confident.

Certain decisions, of course, such as on a multimillion-dollar investment or negotiations with a foreign government, are made in Osaka. Even so, senior executives at headquarters have to be on the same wavelength as our people abroad. A quick visit is the best way to get a feel for local realities. During my tenure as president I made more than sixty trips overseas.

Fascinating People

My three meetings with Singapore Prime Minister Lee Kuan

Yew, a strong leader determined to industrialize his city-state, were memorable. The first time was in 1978, when I called on him to explain Matsushita Electric's position on some matter. Delighted at my candor, he invited me to visit again when I was in Singapore. On another occasion, he asked my opinion about whether foreign subsidiaries would leave if his government raised workers' wages. The populace had endured poverty long enough and deserved a higher standard of living, the prime minister said, but he feared the multinational corporations would move elsewhere to cut labor costs.

When the yen began to appreciate rapidly against the U.S. dollar, we decided to increase production at our Singapore plant and added a third shift. During a meeting with the prime minister, I informed him of this. He was pleased and said U.S. corporations had complained that they were unable to run three shifts. Now he could cite Matsushita Electric to show that it could be done.

Our meetings were cordial and informal, with just the prime minister and I present. He listened attentively and I came away with a sense of why Singapore is one of the strongest among the Newly Industrializing Economies (NIEs). The prime minister reportedly exhorts his subordinates with Confucian-like slogans: "Give Clear Signals and Be Consistent," "Stay Clean: Dismiss the Venal," "Win Respect, Not Popularity," "Spread Benefits: Don't Deprive the People," "Strive to Succeed: Never Give Up."

Of my three visits to Indonesia, the second, in 1984, is etched in my memory because it involved a remarkable man, the late Dr. Th. M. Gobel. He was chairman of a joint venture, P. T. National Gobel, a prominent politician, and founder of the Matsushita Gobel Foundation's Education and Training Center, which was designed to groom managers for the next stage of Indonesia's industrialization. Gobel had moved heaven and earth to establish the center, and I went for the dedication ceremony.

He had been in Tokyo the year before for treatment of diabetes. When I visited him in the hospital, he told me his doctor had recommended an operation. "I'm too old. This is the body I was born with and I'll take it to the grave the way it is," he said. Changing the subject, he said, "Construction has finally started on the center. I don't know if I'll live long enough to see it open next year, but I want you to attend." With tears in his eyes, he also asked me to look after his oldest son, Rachmat, who was studying at a Japanese university. Gobel was grooming the lad to take over the family business and be, like himself, a bridge between Indonesia and Japan.

I arrived in Jakarta a day before the ceremony and went directly from the airport to Gobel's home. Gravely ill, he got out of bed, sat in a chair, and thanked me profusely for coming. After the dedication, I called Gobel and told him that everything had gone smoothly and his dream was now a reality. I intended to give him a detailed report in person the next day, but he died that night. Indonesians mourned the loss of this distinguished leader. President Suharto and his cabinet were among the many dignitaries who attended his funeral.

Rachmat Gobel is still studying in Japan. A diligent young man, he delivered newspapers to earn spending money and is determined to follow in his father's footsteps. People like this father-and-son team are invaluable friends of Japan.

Feminine Ambassadors

Japanese businessmen overseas are often criticized for their clannishness, withdrawing from the local community and socializing exclusively with one another. Japanese-only golfing get-togethers have earned foreign anger. We are sometimes our own worst enemy.

Only in recent years did I begin to appreciate the crucial role wives play in an overseas assignment. In some countries, drinking water must be boiled and vegetables carefully washed before eating. Wives have to be sanitation engineers, cooks, and nurses, too. A family's failure to adjust to a different language and unfamiliar customs can distract a Matsushita Electric employee to the point where he can't function on the job.

Children adapt easily to a new culture, make friends quickly, and often don't want to leave when their father's tour of duty is over. They may balk at spicy food or miss a favorite Japanese dessert for a while, but they soon learn the local language and find substitutes. Wives have more serious adjustment problems, and some are unhappy from the day they arrive until they are back in Japan again.

Several years ago Matsushita Electric began an orientation program for wives going overseas in order to dispel their fears and put them in a positive frame of mind. The supervisor says he can often spot people with potential problems. It's not just a question of whether the women have had contact with foreigners before. Many Japanese wives live within a small circle of family and relatives and are not accustomed to socializing with outsiders. Thrust into an unfamiliar environment with strangers and different mores, they may be overwhelmed. Culture shock can reveal the introverted side of the Japanese female psyche, a shyness that makes them unable to relax and interact with people they don't know. I know of cases where the fate of a whole subsidiary hinged on the ability of the senior Japanese executive's wife to cope.

Some misunderstandings leave you uncertain whether to laugh or cry. The Swiss, for example, train their pet dogs not to bark at strangers. A Japanese family living in Switzerland had a dog who barked at everyone, and the neighbors complained.

"I discipline the dog. I punish it for barking," the wife insisted. "But you do it in Japanese. That's why it doesn't obey!" an angry neighbor retorted. Regardless of whether Swiss dogs don't respond to Japanese commands, imagine that poor wife's embarrassment. Wanting only to blend in inconspicuously, she had become the talk of the neighborhood. The Japanese will have to learn that the Swiss take peace and quiet seriously.

To build a house in Switzerland, a long-time resident told me, you must first post a blueprint in the city hall that specifies the dwelling's size, floor plan, window locations, and the color of the roof and walls. Neighbors can veto features that clash with other dwellings. This is also true for gardens and shrubs, which must be both visually attractive and free of destructive insects or harmful pollens. Swiss towns have a picture-book charm and cleanliness because everybody follows these rules. Japanese neighborhoods are higgledy-piggledy by comparison; builders need only comply with certain structural and safety regulations (some don't even do that). A preference for tidiness or diversity is a matter of taste and values. Japan will need more self-discipline if we want to preserve cityscapes and landscapes, for example, as tourist attractions.

Many Japanese wives are wonderful representatives of Matsushita Electric. In 1980, I attended a celebration of P. T. National Gobel's tenth anniversary. After the ceremony, a chorus of employee wives, Japanese and Indonesian, all in national costume, sang popular songs from both countries. The pronunciation and harmony were so good that with your eyes closed you wouldn't have known they were from different nations. Many hours of practice went into the performance, but, most important, among the women themselves differences of nationality and culture gave way to friendship. It was sisterhood through song.

Music knows no national boundaries, they say, and Japanese songs are very popular in Southeast Asia. I once heard what seemed like a familiar melody and later discovered it was "*Seto no hanayome*," a popular Japanese ballad about a young bride. Singapore even broadcasts NHK's annual New Year's Eve songfest.

About two hundred Japanese live in Dar es Salaam, and the twenty-four school-age children attend the International School there. The school is a little United Nations, with all instruction in English. The twenty-five third graders, for example, hail from eighteen countries: Japan, the United States, Canada, Britain, West Germany, Holland, Denmark, Sweden, Norway, Finland, India, Pakistan, Yemen, Egypt, Sudan, Kenya, Zambia, and Zimbabwe.

Japanese and French children also attend special schools to learn their own languages. One day I stopped in at the Japanese school, which is divided into an upper- and a lower-level class. The students also receive extra math lessons there. Paper is hard to get in Tanzania, and the teacher uses an improvised blackboard, but the kids love the classes. Blissfully unaware of their parents' concern for their safety—in case of injury, medical care is inadequate—the kids run noisily around the school playground.

The teacher had the pupils sketch me. Drawn in simple, bold strokes without artifice, the pictures do bear a certain resemblance. I treasure them as some of my finest souvenirs.

One student, Seiko, is mentioned in *Sights and Sounds of Africa* by Masataka Ito, African correspondent for the *Asahi Shimbun*. Seiko was then in eighth grade and the oldest child in the school. Ito describes how she looked after the younger pupils and helped her mother at home. Seiko made many friends at the International School. She hadn't lost touch with Japan, however; she named her puppies after her favorite foods: "Chikuwa" (fish paste rolls), "Kamaboko" (steamed fish loaf), and "Ganmodoki" (deep-fried tofu balls). Now a college senior in Japan, Seiko reportedly is saving money from a part-time job to return to Tanzania someday.

Hospitality in Rabbit Hutches

As Japan's economic and political role grows, more foreigners—business executives, exchange students, government officials—have come here to work and study. We are considerate hosts, I think, but some forms of hospitality are impossible. We can't invite people to our homes, for example. American businessmen expect the CEO of a major corporation to have a palatial house with at least a swimming pool, but Japanese businessmen don't live on that scale.

One company president—I'll call him Tamura—took an American executive to an exclusive restaurant. The American complained: "You always bring me to splendid, expensive places like this, but sometime I wish you would just invite me to your home." Tamura, realizing that he seemed inhospitable and not wanting to offend a valued client, took the guest to his house after dinner. Unfortunately, Tamura's wife had gone to bed early with a bad cold, so he asked his driver to serve them tea. After a while, the American said, "I've seen enough of the chauffeur's house, Tamura-san. Can we go to your place now?" There isn't much you can say in that situation.

I had a similar experience with a group of British journalists in Kyoto. I invited them to Tsuruya, a famous restaurant built in the old Kyoto style of architecture. Because of the unpretentious exterior, it looks like a private house. We were using the huge second-floor banquet room where foreign leaders and royalty have dined. As we entered the room, a journalist said, "Mr. Yamashita, your villa is fantastic!"

The president of Matsushita Electric's sales agency in Saudi Arabia once complained about my lack of hospitality, telling a Japanese magazine interviewer, "On Mr. Yamashita's first visit to Saudi Arabia I entertained him at my home. I've been to Japan several times, but he has not once reciprocated."

In Saudi Arabia's male-dominated society, dining is an inelegant adventure endured without the help of a stiff drink or feminine companionship. Men sit in a circle on a rug and tear off pieces of meat from a roasting sheep. Afterwards, everyone takes turns puffing on a water pipe, a communal ritual to enhance friendship.

Before my first Saudi Arabian dinner, a Japanese employee warned me, "There will be a sheep's eye. This *pièce de résis-*

tance is served to the guest of honor. Today, that is you, so please eat it. That will impress the host and help our business."

In due course the delicacy was presented. It looked like a fish eye, only twice as big. The sight of that opaque blob staring up at me made me nauseous. If there had been some whisky, I would have closed my eyes, swallowed the slimy orb, and washed it down with a tumbler of Scotch. Coca-Cola wasn't quite the chaser I needed. To make a long story short, I failed the test and declined the honor of a sheep's eye.

Another aspect of Japanese entertaining that puzzles foreigners is the absence of wives. Several Americans have said, "I know many Japanese businessmen, but I've never met a single wife." As a friendship develops, Americans expect to meet a colleague's wife and children, to get to know the whole family, and they feel uncomfortable when it doesn't happen.

Appreciating the Differences

When Japanese children in an elementary school art class in France drew the sun as a red ball, French kids called the drawings "weird" and laughed. The Japanese see the sun as red, and there is a set phrase, "the crimson sun." But to the French it seems yellow. I suppose the scientific explanation is that the sun looks different in Japan's humid atmosphere compared to France's drier climate. Climate would also explain why in the Middle East the sun sometimes appears to be pure white.

Etiquette also varies from place to place. A South Korean woman—let's call her Ms. Kim—was coming to a Japanese university to study, and her parents arranged for her to board with the family of a Japanese acquaintance, whom I shall call Watanabe. This arrangement would place their daughter in safe, wholesome surroundings, they thought, and expose her to the lifestyle of a Japanese family as well.

Mrs. Watanabe was solicitous and helpful, but at dinner she suddenly said to Ms. Kim, "Please lift the rice bowl up to your mouth." The Korean woman was embarrassed and upset. In South Korea, it is considered impolite to raise the rice bowl to your lips, the exact opposite of Japanese custom. For this reason, Korean tables are higher than those in Japan. To the annoyance of her young guest, Mrs. Watanabe insisted she eat in the Japanese way. The Japanese have to appreciate that what we consider good form, people elsewhere, even in a country as geographically close as South Korea, may regard as odd or crude. We have to beware of ethnocentrism.

Westerners often say, "The Japanese don't give a clear yes or no. They equivocate with expressions like, 'I'll have to think it over.'" Compared with European and American frankness, this vagueness is old-fashioned, they say. The Western assumption that Japan won't be internationalized until we become direct and unequivocal is itself a culture-bound notion. Many other peoples also avoid negative responses.

The Filipinos, for example, will often bend the truth to spare another person's feelings; a direct no is even rarer there than in Japan. One day the maid for a Japanese household announced she had to quit because her mother was ill. Although distressed at losing a good servant on short notice, the wife gave her some money to help with the medical expenses and wished her good luck. A few days later the Japanese woman discovered that the maid had gone to work for another family nearby for higher pay. The story had been a white lie. The maid wasn't embarrassed when they met on the street; on the contrary, it was the Japanese wife who felt somehow guilty.

Many cultures avoid or defer conflict by subtle methods. "A soft answer turneth away wrath," says the Bible. Western clarity is just one approach. The Japanese must be attuned to whatever society they find themselves in.

The Burden of Affluence

Rapid appreciation of the yen, especially since the autumn of

1985, has caused serious problems for Japanese manufacturers. By rigorous cost-cutting we adjusted to a 10 percent to 20 percent rise in the currency's value, but the 40 percent jump pushed many firms to the edge.

Japan's huge current account surpluses triggered the yen's surge. They rose from $20 billion in 1983 to $35 billion the next year, to $50 billion in 1985. By comparison, during OPEC's heyday in the 1970s, the oil-producing countries' total surplus was only $40 billion.

Accumulation of such surpluses by one country endangers the global economy, and Japan will be hurt most by restrictions on free trade. Many of our trading partners regard us as a rogue nation that ruthlessly floods the world with exports. Actually, West Germany sells more abroad than Japan, but huge imports have kept its overall surplus at a tolerable level and avoided the criticism directed at Tokyo. The Germans export Mercedes-Benz's, but they buy medium-priced autos from France and the United States. Strong sales of German beer are offset by purchases of British Scotch whisky and French wine. Bonn's trade policy is carefully crafted to maximize comparative advantage and prevent imbalances.

In Japan's case, however, 60 percent of imports are raw materials, oil, and natural gas. Our industrial structure makes it difficult to increase purchases of foreign manufactured goods; inexpensive, quality products are already available from domestic manufacturers. In 1985, a blue ribbon commission—the Advisory Group on Economic Structural Adjustment for International Harmony—led by Haruo Maekawa, former president of the Bank of Japan, called for a shift from an export-oriented economy to one driven by domestic demand. Investment in housing, roads, and expanded leisure does stimulate consumer spending, but the putative priorities ran into an immutable reality: Japan's land shortage. Spiraling land prices in Tokyo—almost 85.7 percent in 1986 alone—put affordable housing beyond the reach of most people. Domestic demand is not a panacea.

If neither exports nor domestic demand can be increased, manufacturers will have no alternative but to move production offshore. This poses the danger of de-industrialization, but at least Japanese factories will provide jobs in the host countries and be safely inside protectionist barriers.

Our powerful economy has had a much greater impact on the world than most Japanese appreciate. We caused these dislocations so it is up to us to find solutions. Japan's problem is that our manufacturing sector has been too successful, whereas the United States is troubled by declining competitiveness. We can't stand idly by when our best customer is in trouble.

We have long regarded the world as a series of markets to capture. This economic tunnel vision has skewered our perspective on global issues and Japan's role in the world community. As a nation, our behavior has often been disruptive and our policies on trade liberalization and development halfhearted and inadequate.

There is more to existence than a trillion-dollar GNP and a work ethic, but I fear many Japanese have little interest in the finer things in life. Conversations with foreign businessmen range from music and art to history; the average Japanese corporate employee talks about his job, business conditions, and golf. Having achieved material affluence, the Japanese must now cultivate the garden of their soul.

6
A Second Life

Each passing year brings retirement a bit closer, that point in life when we must make way for the next generation. To men who have worked thirty years or more for the same company, the thought of being cut off from colleagues at the office or plant is a chilling prospect. Nevertheless, everyone must step down sometime, so it's best to prepare yourself psychologically. With careful planning, there can be a life after work.

Some Japanese men regard retirement with the dread of a condemned prisoner facing the guillotine, while others can hardly wait to start a new life. As I mentioned earlier, I used to meet informally with employees about to retire. Each month, there were fifteen or sixteen, nearly all men, and I think they were fairly candid about their feelings toward the company.

Many were not prepared for retirement, especially management-level personnel who often panicked about a year before the fateful date. That wasn't enough time to prepare adequately. Although factory employees got ready in various ways, managers were afraid people would say, "He seems to be already making plans for his retirement," implying that he was no longer serious about his job. Many executives had such a strong work ethic and a sense of corporate loyalty that they would have felt guilty if they had looked beyond Matsushita Electric to the future. Their personal identity had become submerged in the corporation.

Even as a young employee I built a wall, or at least a fence, between myself and the company. I tried to keep my overtime to a minimum. The hours after work were my time, and I used them to read and broaden my knowledge. I didn't let Matsushita Electric and its problems intrude into this private sphere. I enjoyed holidays, for example, whereas many Japanese equate relaxation and time off with absenteeism. The workaholic—a person who stays late every night or takes a full briefcase home—burns out. In long-distance running, one of my hobbies, you learn the importance of pacing yourself. Dedication is fine; compulsive-obsessive zeal is self-destructive. Ever since high school, I have believed a person needs outside interests.

Setting goals is the first step to accomplishing them. An objective focuses the mind and rallies the spirit. The adrenalin starts to flow. Mountain climbing is one of my avocations. When I decide to climb a peak overseas, I do considerable homework, reading as much about it as I can and consulting with people who have already climbed the mountain. It's fun to prepare a careful assault plan. Personal interests help you keep your job in perspective and cope with change. Everyone needs a private agenda and the free time to carry it out.

The employees retiring now were born in the 1920s and came of age during World War II or just afterwards. Caught up in wartime mobilization or postwar privation and recovery, they never learned how to enjoy leisure time. This generation was in their thirties and forties during Japan's period of rapid economic growth, and they deferred vacations and worked brutally long hours. Perhaps this explains their lack of foresight about retirement.

In recent years retirees seem more pleased with the financial benefits they get than they used to, thanks in part to the company's enormous growth. Some have told me, "I never dreamed I would be this well off." When they joined us in the late 1940s or during the Korean War in the early 1950s, we were a small, struggling firm. Who could have foreseen that today Matsushita Electric would be one of Japan's most profitable corporations?

Planning for Retirement

Mandatory retirement at Matsushita Electric is at age sixty, about average for Japan. As president I tried, in a modest way, to alleviate apprehension about the post-retirement years. A corporation owes that to its people and to society.

In 1979, management and the union conducted parallel surveys of our employees to determine preferences about retirement. The questionnaires included such queries as, "Do you want to continue working after age sixty?" Those who answered in the affirmative were asked, "What is your primary reason?" In the company survey, 82 percent of the respondents said they wanted to continue working (the figure was 79 percent in the union poll). One might have guessed this result: most people would rather keep busy than watch TV all day.

Of the respondents who wanted to stay on the job, some felt they were too young to be put out to pasture. There were comments like, "I know my field inside out. I'm much more competent than the younger men." But most of the "continue-working" respondents cited concern about living on a lower income.

With the union we established a Post-Retirement Policy Committee. In 1981, we set up a Retirement Counseling Center and a set of options that enables employees to work past sixty. Generally, the new arrangements are as follows. Blue-collar employees can retire at sixty or sixty-five provided they make the choice when they are fifty-five. White-collar personnel have an option to work a part-time "flex-time" system—two or three days a week, mornings or afternoons; they have to decide whether to do so at age sixty. The Retirement Options Plan has proved very popular with some personnel. A patent specialist, for example, who can prepare a brief on a new invention after a quick review of the relevant foreign-language documents, can continue to use his hard-earned knowledge and is invaluable to the company as a consultant. Media publicity brought many inquiries about the plan from other companies.

To our surprise, however, at first only about 30 percent of eligible employees opted to work until sixty-five (the figure later rose to 45 percent), a far cry from the roughly 80 percent indicated in our survey. One reason for the disparity is Matsushita Electric's new pension system. Previously, employees received a lump-sum severance payment based on salary and length of service. Now an equivalent amount is placed in a company-managed pension fund and retirees receive monthly payments. With this money and social security benefits, most people have enough income to live in modest comfort. The husband can stop working and enjoy himself.

Some employees who hoped to become consultants for other firms after retiring from Matsushita had second thoughts. A personnel officer was approached by an expanding medium-sized company that needed his expertise, but he rejected the offer, saying, "Personnel work is the one thing I don't want to do." After decades of dealing with promotions and transfers, he didn't want to hear any more hard-luck stories or complaints.

Retirement Abroad

Some retirees lead active, interesting lives thanks to a positive attitude and planning. They are proof that youth is a state of mind, not a matter of how many years you've been on this planet. One of our salesmen, a man who spent several years in Mexico, was always fascinated by China and apparently studied Chinese in his spare time. After retirement, he found a job with a small travel agency, assisting tour groups going to China. His appetite whetted by these visits, he enrolled at Beijing University for formal study of Chinese history and culture. He visited me when I was in Beijing on business, and it was delightful to hear a man in his sixties discuss his studies and future plans. A couple of my acquaintances are studying Pali at a university in Sri Lanka in order to read the Buddhist sutras in the original. By paying a fee, foreigners can obtain permanent residency there. I guess there must be many retired Japanese living abroad.

A former Matsushita Electric engineer is sitting in on philosophy classes at a university in Japan. He has always had an active, inquiring mind, and now he has the time to let it roam among the great thinkers of East and West. Another acquaintance took up painting after retiring, although he had never held a brush in his hand before. It's as if he had been blind all his life and was seeing landscapes for the first time, he says. By trying to reproduce these scenes, he has gained an appreciation of nature. A special gleam comes into his eye when he talks about painting, and I must say I envy him.

It's wonderful to see people making the most of their retirement instead of withering into elderly couch potatoes. Yet the great majority of men in their sixties stop thinking of new challenges and slip into a quiet rut. I don't mean to be critical, for after thirty or forty years of hard work, they deserve to take life easy. But what about their wives? Will the wife be content with a husband who is home all the time and expects to be waited on hand and foot? During their working life most Japanese men are married to their company and neglect their spouses. A total commitment to the job leaves little time or energy for family life. A husband's retirement is thus often traumatic for the wife: family income dips and a virtual stranger is around the house interrupting her routine. Many women wish there were day-care centers for retired husbands, a place where they could be parked from nine in the morning till six at night. Wives don't want to give up their interests and friends to become full-time maids.

A well-known business leader told me about his marital situation. He and his wife have had a reasonably good relationship, but now that the children are grown up and gone, their marriage seems empty. They have nothing to talk about; meals are eaten in silence. When the children were at home, conversation centered on their activities: "Yoshimi's late today. Is he still at his after-school lessons?" or "Kimie seems to like that fellow Tsutomu." When the kids left, the couple had no interests in common. Each felt uncomfortable and awkward around the other. Recognizing the crisis, they decided to do something about it, and began going places together—to the movies, to Kabuki, and to hot-spring resorts.

A husband and wife who haven't really talked to each other in years don't suddenly become sparkling conversationalists or good listeners. As a couple gets older, each tends to take the other for granted. Appreciative comments or signs of affection seem like too much trouble. Able to see only their spouse's faults, some husbands and wives complain and criticize constantly. The partner, bored and resentful of this negative patter, withdraws into silence.

A company president once told me of a couple who saw the danger signs and came up with a novel solution. They put a little doll on the dining-room table and directed critical remarks to it. In a typical scenario the husband says, "Mother seems to be in a bad mood tonight." The wife replies, "Tell him I've been busy all day and I'm tired." The doll is a neutral intermediary. Each can speak freely; neither resents criticism addressed to a third party. Perhaps other couples, especially of my generation, can use this method to bridge the conversation gap.

Youth Is a State of Mind

Stepping down in February 1986 was liberation day for me. My assumptions before I became a CEO about the freedom of action I would enjoy had proved naive. There were complaints about my mountain climbing, which were to some extent understandable. But I found that I couldn't stop in at an ordinary bar or eating place after work. When I had run the air conditioner division, I had done so regularly, but as president my old haunts were off-limits. I didn't want VIP treatment, of course, but the owners made a fuss over me. Alerted to my position, other patrons became uncomfortable: I might know their boss or the president of their company.

Now I'm free. The next few years are my real youth, and I'm going to do what I want: climb mountains and play Go against all comers. Deferred adventures have given me stored-up energy. I feel like an American college student heading for Ft. Lauderdale on spring break. It's time to sow a few mature oats. This is not to suggest that I was a prisoner in the board room or had an unhappy youth. I've enjoyed each stage of my life in different ways, but today, divested of a CEO's responsibilities, I'm free of all care. That phrase is usually associated with undergraduates, but the meaning is qualitatively better at my age. Immune to callow mistakes, I can enjoy life to the hilt.

The inspirational philosophy of John W. Lewis, based on the poem "Youth" by Samuel Ullman (1840–1911), expresses my feelings perfectly.

> Youth is not a time of life—it is a state of mind; it is a temper of the will, a quality of the imagination, a vigor of the emotions, a predominance of courage over timidity, of the appetite for adventure over love of ease.
>
> Nobody grows old by merely living a number of years; people grow old only by deserting their ideals. Years wrinkle the skin, but to give up enthusiasm wrinkles the soul. Worry, doubt, self-distrust, fear and despair—these are the long, long years that bow the head and turn the growing spirit back to dust.

About twenty years ago, Mr. Matsushita said something

similar. Later I learned that he had written a poem, based in part on Ullman's, and made it a personal motto.

Youth is youngness at heart.
Youth is eternal for those
Who are full of faith and hope
And greet the challenges of each new day
With courage and confidence.

To me, youthfulness means setting goals and throwing yourself into accomplishing them. As CEO, work had to take top priority. Any mountain climbing or game of Go I squeezed into my schedule were just brief diversions from business problems. A desk piled high with market research and production statistics always awaited me the next morning. Although I still have some minor duties as an executive advisor, essentially my time is my own. I'm free to try anything. It's a fantastic feeling to be able to say, "What shall I do next?"

I equate meeting challenges with youthfulness. The antithesis is the "better safe than sorry" mentality. I'm curious about the world around me, what the twenty-first century will be like. It would be fascinating to live in Africa for a while: to see nature in the raw, undefiled by so-called civilization, and to know the good-natured people there and experience the unhurried tempo of life. From brief business trips to Africa, I can understand why Japanese who have worked there speak of it so fondly and want to go back. Perhaps the lure of that great, mysterious continent proves that I still have a youthful spirit.

"Because They Are There"

People often ask me, "Why are you so crazy about mountain climbing?" and I'm at a loss to explain. "Does the physical exertion make you feel good," a friend will persist, "or is it standing there above the clouds?" But only a mountain climber can appreciate the feeling. Trite as it may sound, I guess the only answer to, "Why do you climb mountains?" is, "Because they are there."

Trudging up a steep path with a heavy backpack is hard work. Often I think to myself, "This is a stupid way to spend a Saturday afternoon." But when you reach the top, there is an exhilarating sense of accomplishment. You forget the heat, your twisted ankle, and your blisters, and begin to think about the next mountain!

Running the marathon is like mountain climbing, a battle against pain and fatigue. That's the point: to endure. Nothing matches the elation of pushing yourself to the limit and staying the course. Accepting difficult new work assignments is another way of testing yourself. There's no fun in doing the same easy job forever.

In the summer of 1986, my wife and I climbed the three mountains at Tateyama in Toyama Prefecture for the fifth time. It's one of our favorite places, and we plan to return every summer. We "camp out" in a hotel at Murodo, a plateau formed of lava. It is an unbeatable combination: good food and wine, and alpine hiking. Many older people climb the Tateyama peaks, and recently we even met an eighty-year-old couple on the slopes. My wife and I felt like young whippersnappers.

My interest in mountains dates from reading a book by the writer Hisaya Fukada, *Great Japanese Mountains*, in which he described places he had climbed. It was so popular that Fukada wrote a sequel, *Great Mountains Abroad*. Although he didn't actually climb all the forty-one peaks he described, Fukada used the same criteria in choosing them as he had applied in Japan—beauty, history, and unique features.

From Fukada's book I picked several reasonable climbs abroad. My criteria were accessibility to the foot of the mountain by vehicle and a relatively easy trek to the top. A third consideration was a Matsushita Electric plant in the area for local logistical support. My short list was: Mt. Kinabalu, Sabah,

Malaysia; Mt. Damavand, Iran; Mt. Popocatepetl, Mexico; and Mt. Kilimanjaro, Tanzania.

I climbed Mt. Kinabalu (13,431 feet) in 1975. The local people regard it with awe as a sacred place of the dead. Shrouded in clouds, the fantastic crags soaring skyward are never fully visible, adding to its mystique.

I drove from Kota Kinabalu, a port and the capital of Sabah (formerly North Borneo), to the foot of the mountain in about three hours. After a light lunch, I was ready. The party consisted of myself, a male guide, and two female porters, who were the guide's daughters. The local people are small; the two girls were fourteen and fifteen, but looked no more than ten. They wore rubber sandals and I wondered if they would be able to keep their footing in the rough parts. But they carried the loads all the way without mishap. Although traveling light, I was soon huffing and puffing as we walked through the thick undergrowth and started up the slope. Tall trees blocked out the sun; in midafternoon, the path was dark. We went slowly so I could gradually become accustomed to the altitude, but nevertheless above the 10,000-foot mark, I found it difficult to breathe, whereas the teen-age porters had no problems.

The guide didn't speak English. Occasionally, I said "Shindoi na," which means "I'm bushed" in Japanese. He understood and stopped for a short break. By nightfall we reached the Panaraban Cabin at 11,000 feet. The plan was for me to stay there, while the guide and his daughters used a hut nearby. We would climb to the summit the next morning. I was to be alone in the shelter, surrounded by a deep, eerie silence.

I closed the door firmly, crawled into my sleeping bag, and fell into an exhausted sleep, only to be awakened suddenly a few hours later by the sound of a raging torrent. Rain pelts the higher levels of Mt. Kinabalu almost nightly and rushes down the granite rocks like a waterfall.

I thought I heard a knock on the door, but the rain made it

difficult to hear. Then there was a voice! Remembering that the peak was supposedly sacred to the dead, for an instant I feared an evil spirit had come to drive out the Japanese infidel. Then I thought it's this spooky place and my imagination. But the knocking and voices persisted. I got up and nervously opened the door. The guide's daughters were standing there, drenched to the skin. I let them in and tried to find out what had happened. By sign language they indicated that the rain had flooded their hut, though their father had decided to stick it out there. Gallantry required an offer of refuge. The three of us tried to get some rest, but to my dismay they snored like buzz saws! I'm happy to report that we survived the night, although not quite as snug as peas in a pod, and reached the summit, Ross Peak, the next morning.

Mt. Damavand

Japanese have nicknamed Mt. Damavand (18,602 feet) "Iran's Mt. Fuji." Like our most famous mountain, the dormant volcano is the country's highest peak and is always capped with snow. It's the major crag of the Elburz range that stretches south along the Caspian. I climbed it on July 30, 1978.

A Japanese engineer briefed me beforehand. He was one of three men from a Japan International Cooperation Agency team of communication specialists working on a project in Iran who had climbed Mt. Damavand in 1975. Very few Japanese have made the ascent. The Iran Mountaineering Association also provided information and arranged for a guide who was familiar with most of Iran's peaks and had climbed in the Himalayas. Mindful of my amateur status, he planned the expedition very carefully. We took the relatively easy southern approach to avoid the sharp precipices on the northeastern route.

The Japanese engineer told me there was a stone hut used by nomads at the 10,000-foot level. A family of sheepherders lived there in the summer and had given his group delicious fresh goat milk. The trio had taken a picture of the family and asked me to deliver a copy. I agreed but wondered if nomads would be in the same place three years later.

The old man and his family were still there and just as friendly, and they were delighted with the photo. Their home was a hole in a cliff, about ten feet square, with a pile of stones at the entrance serving as a makeshift door. Living there on that mountainside, raising goats much as their ancestors had for centuries, these nice people seemed beyond time and space.

I had some goat's milk and it tasted great, perhaps because of the altitude, and I felt tremendously refreshed. Afterwards, I watched one of the children milk a goat. He squeezed the milk into a bucket and then poured it into a jug. I noticed black lumps on the bottom of the bucket and asked what they were. "Sheep dung," my guide said. That gave me pause about a refill, but, nevertheless, that first glass hit the spot.

My guide and I stayed in an untended hut at the 13,000-foot level. The night sky was breathtaking—a canopy of glittering diamonds spread on black velvet. It seemed as if I could reach out and scoop up a handful.

We started for the top at four the next morning but ran into trouble at 16,500 feet—sulphur gas. At about 18,000 feet the fumes were so strong that I could hardly breathe. The stones and boulders were stained a yellowish green. The spectacular beauty of the night before had given way to a scene from Dante's *Inferno*. To make matters worse, my head was throbbing from the altitude. The summit was within view but I didn't think I could make it. Gasping, one short step at a time, I finally plodded to the top.

Other Climbs

Taiwan has about one hundred mountains in the 10,000-foot class (Japan has only fourteen). In climbing about ten of them,

I've rarely met anyone. The government of Taiwan encourages students to hike and climb as part of a national fitness program, but young people only head for the slopes during school vacations. I have climbed Mt. Yushan (13,113 feet), Taiwan's highest peak, four times now. On the second occasion, in August 1984, my wife and I went together (with one guide), and we didn't meet a soul along the way. In Malaysia and Iran, too, you rarely encounter a local climber. Nearly all the hikers are Europeans.

Compared to mountain huts overseas, those in Japan tend to be dirty and strewn with trash. Maybe it's because there are so many climbers in Japan, and as a people we aren't fastidious about public places. Discarded food cartons and soda cans blight our parks and beaches, too. Another factor is that the Japanese eat the same food on a climb as they do in their daily lives, and so these meals involve a lot of ingredients—and a lot of packages.

In recent years I've taken my wife, Kikuko, with me on several climbs. The first time, Mt. Fuji in 1980, she dropped out midway because she was exhausted before we started. We took the night train from Osaka on a Friday after I finished work and didn't start the ascent till Saturday afternoon. On subsequent climbs, however, she has held up much better than I. Kikuko was a great help on Mt. Yushan, carrying a full pack all the way. It's very good to have someone who remembers to bring the aspirin when you have a splitting headache at 13,000 feet. She always loved to walk and now is an enthusiastic convert to doing it uphill. Her motto is: "Have pack, will travel."

The Osaka business community took a dim view of my "dangerous" hobby. A senior business leader took me aside one day and said, "You have to consider your position. What if you got killed? You can't take risks like that." I reassured him and others that I would "cease and desist from such reckless behavior," or words to that effect. I didn't stop, of course. But thereafter I kept the company informed.

My associates seemed particularly troubled by the fact that I often went with just my wife and not a large group. I prefer traveling as a couple because if one of us gets tired or twists an ankle, we just head back. That would disrupt a large party's plans; someone would insist on accompanying us. To avoid ruining the group's outing, we might continue on the climb despite an injury. I've been in such situations several times, most memorably on my nemesis, Mt. Popocatepetl (17,887 feet).

I've attacked this peak twice and failed both times. In November 1979, I planned to sleep in a cabin at 13,000 feet and reach the summit the next morning. I got up during the night to use the toilet and, in the pitch dark, wandered into the generator room by mistake and tripped over the machinery. The result was a sprained ankle, a ridiculous accident that ended the climb for me.

I tried again in November 1983. Too much tequila at a send-off party the night before doomed this attempt. I made it to the same cabin, but that was the end of the road. A terrible hangover compounded by altitude sickness did me in. Mt. Popocatepetl is an unlucky giant for me.

Being on your own gives you the flexibility to change plans. With a group, everyone has to follow the consensus. I know my limits and never push myself too far or take chances. A lone-wolf style is the safest way for me.

Mt. Kilimanjaro (19,340 feet), the highest peak in Africa, still lies ahead. The fine paths and many shelters make it accessible to anyone with a little climbing experience. Thanks to the strong yen, many young Japanese jet off to Tanzania over the year-end holidays. Kinji Imanishi, the famed ecologist and explorer, has said that even women and kids can climb the "shining peak." On the other hand, a Japanese university mountaineering club classifies it as dangerous. No matter how user-friendly a mountain seems, climbers shouldn't take it for granted.

Most mountains have a zigzag route to the top and climbers gradually get used to the altitude. Mt. Kilimanjaro's direct ascent can be traumatic. Some people make it to the top easily, but then have to be carried down on stretchers. Curiously, this seems to happen more to seasoned mountaineers than neophytes.

In 1985, a Matsushita group—five men and one woman, all about thirty years old—scaled Mt. Kilimanjaro. Perhaps the males were worried about their "weaker" companion and carried her pack. Whatever the explanation, afterwards the men could barely walk, but the woman felt fine.

I mentioned this incident to a professional female climber, who said women can be honest about their feelings and say, "I'm fagged out." There is no psychological pressure. Men, however, have to live up to a macho image. They feel they must be in charge—leaders—and literally wear themselves out. She may be right.

Mountains and Stress

I am often asked, "Does mountain climbing make you a better manager?" My standard reply is, "I'm so exhausted when I go on a climb that I don't think about my job or whether my managerial skills are being enhanced." That's the truth. I concentrate completely on the path, on making sure that the next tired step isn't off the cliff. At the top, I just want to rest, have a cup of Japanese green tea, and look around. It's not that I consciously put the company out of my mind; when I start up a peak I just forget about Osaka, new products, and the yen's appreciation. For me, mountain climbing is the best cure for stress, a strenuous alternative to valium, anti-ulcer drugs, and the rest of the pharmacopeia often found in an executive's desk drawer.

I don't find golf relaxing. Playing with business associates, I spend much of the time looking for errant drives or blasting away in a sand trap. It always seems as if I'm slowing up the game and embarrassing the others. Golf is too stressful for me. In fact, I've developed a defensive strategy. I arrange for our foursome to be first off the tee and we finish the course by noon. After lunch, I go home, take a nap or read, and recover from the morning's "relaxation." Otherwise, I would be exhausted at the office the next day.

Travel for pleasure is another antidote to stress. The excitement, romance if you will, of taking a superexpress train or a jet helps to put the office behind me. Maybe the motion shakes my thoughts out of the business rut. I prefer not to travel with Matsushita colleagues because they are an unwitting reminder of work. It's wonderful to be someplace like a mountaintop without a telephone so you can't call the office about that "urgent" matter.

In the summer of 1985, Minoru Morita, managing director of Matsushita Electric, was killed in a traffic accident. I was at Tateyama and had just returned to the hotel at Murodo after hours of tramping around the mountains when someone telephoned with the news. Still in my hiking outfit and exhilarated by the scenery and clean air, the tragedy seemed part of a different world that had nothing to do with me. For an instant I wasn't even shocked. Then the impact of the terrible loss, to me personally and to the company, sunk in and I immediately returned to Osaka.

I mention this sad event as an example of how physical separation from our everyday milieu can thrust us into a different spiritual dimension. To be able to switch back instantly to the "real" world is a great gift, which I certainly don't have. Yet in the day-to-day routine of running a corporation, an executive must readjust quickly. I've tried to train myself to concentrate on a problem, give it my best shot, and then forget about it and move on to the next one. You have to slam the door on the hobgoblins of "what if" or "maybe."

Keeping in Touch

As CEO, I was chauffeured everywhere; for nine years I never used public transportation. After I stepped down, I wanted to take the Osaka subway one day and couldn't find it! What an embarrassment for someone who for decades had been a strap-hanger on trains, buses, and subways. Another time after leaving the presidency, I was at Hamamatsucho Station in Tokyo and wanted to buy a monorail ticket to Haneda Airport. Out of change, I took a ¥1,000 bill from my wallet and looked for a ticket seller, only to discover that the whole operation had been automated. There were no clerks and the machines only took coins (the new machines accept ¥1,000 notes). Feeling like a country bumpkin on his first visit to the capital, I had to ask a passerby how to purchase a ticket.

An acquaintance, the president of a department store, is also chauffeured everywhere. To avoid losing touch with the public mood and fashion, he makes a point of sometimes riding the subway. I'm finding it's great fun to rediscover the world around me.

A CEO away from the corporate life-support system of secretaries and aides is often like a fish out of water. Several years ago I traveled alone to a consumer electronics conference in Brussels, Belgium. Heavy fog closed the Frankfurt airport and my flight was cancelled. I couldn't notify the conference secretariat because I didn't know where in Brussels the meeting was being held. A limousine always met me at the airport on business trips, and the driver always knew the destination. Usually, I didn't have to bother with such trivia as hotel names and meeting sites.

In exasperation, I called Matsushita Electric in Osaka. Early morning in Frankfurt is evening in Japan: a recorded announcement advised me to try again at 8:30 A.M. There was a flight to Brussels, but, reluctant to use an unfamiliar carrier, I decided to go by train. At the station a Japanese I met agreed to alert the Matsushita Electric office in Brussels of my arrival time. The train was on schedule, but no one was waiting for me. Baffled, I told a taxi driver to take me to the best hotel in the city, reasoning that the conference might be held there.

Wrong again. So I had a desk clerk ask the Japanese Embassy and finally found the meeting. Later I learned that there are two train stations in Brussels, and the Japanese employee assigned to escort me had been waiting at the other one. When I didn't turn up, he called the secretariat and reported me missing. A senior official called him a "world-class idiot" for losing the president of Matsushita Electric. The fallout hit me, too. After this misadventure, Osaka decided that I was not to travel overseas on business by myself.

Traveling alone is marvelously relaxing. Once the plane is airborne, I can read a book or sleep, whatever I feel like. Aides are always oversolicitous, bustling about trying to be helpful. They are bored and I feel like a suspect under surveillance. Nevertheless, it's true that mishaps do befall the solitary traveler in a foreign land. As a young man, I once took the wrong plane and ended up in a strange city. Upon discovering my error, I flew back to my point of departure and started all over again. Flights were not as frequent in those days, so it took me quite a while to get from point A to point B. It was a memorable trip.

Staying Healthy

I used to run every morning. One day a young man in sneakers and a sweat suit was outside my house. He seemed to have been waiting and he ran along behind me. Jogging was a fad then, and I assumed he was a neighbor's son. He showed up several mornings in a row and ran exactly the same route.

"Who are you?" I finally asked. "A newspaper reporter," he said. It was right after my promotion and the media were playing up the "Yamashita leap" over senior directors. His editor's orders were "stick to Yamashita until you find out what makes him tick." One of the journalist's qualifications for the assignment was that he had been a long-distance runner in college. As a cub reporter he probably worked till late at night. Nevertheless, he was in front of my house every morning, bright-eyed and bushy-tailed. I was a serious runner and kept up a fast pace. Gradually, he became less an investigative journalist and more a fitness partner. We were both soaked with perspiration after a run. I felt sorry for him having to go into the office like that and let him shower at my house. Our strange partnership was disrupted when I went on several business trips and he missed a few mornings, too. After that, his editor must have pulled him off the assignment.

Japanese reporters on the scent of a major story are relentless. Forget about your right to privacy; they will be on your doorstep at midnight and six in the morning looking for a lively quote. That morning jogger epitomizes the lengths they will go to for an exclusive.

Now, instead of running every day, I only jog occasionally to get in shape for mountain climbing. About three months before a climb, I jog once or twice a week from my house to Katsuoji Temple in Minoo and back. I start at five, get home by seven, have a shower and a bottle of beer, and head for work feeling great.

In March 1981, unbeknownst to the company, I ran in the Pearl Marathon in Amakusa, Kumamoto Prefecture. I wanted to see if my daily running routine would pay off in a real race, to find out if I could run the whole twenty kilometers. The race was on a Sunday and my wife, who also intended to run, and I flew to Kumamoto the day before. There was no place at the site to check our belongings, so she agreed to stay with them. I ran alone and managed to finish the course. It was a sunny, cloudless day, and I got a bad sunburn, especially on my bald pate, which I tried to cover up the following day at the office.

While I was limbering up before the race, a young woman approached me.

"Aren't you Mr. Yamashita, president of Matsushita Electric? Are you running in the marathon?" she asked.

"How do you know who I am?" I said.

"I saw your name on the entrants' list," she replied.

The woman worked for a local National distributor and, because Matsushita Electric was a sponsor of the event, she happened to look at the runners' names and spotted mine. She had come by to offer a few words of support. I wanted to avoid publicity and the "what-if" reaction in Osaka, so I asked her to tell no one I was there. In return, I posed for a picture with her.

Hobbies

My taste in reading runs to travel, exploration, and mountain climbing. Among my favorite books are *Seven Years in Tibet* by Heinrich Harrer, a German who was interned in India during World War II and escaped to Tibet; Norwegian explorer Roald Amundsen's *The North West Passage: Being the Record of a Voyage of Exploration of the Ship Gjöa, 1903-1907*; and Hisaya Fukada's *Climbing the Himalayas*. I like the excitement and tension of real-life adventures.

My three favorite novelists are Shugoro Yamamoto (1903–67), Jiro Osaragi (1897–1973), and Kuni Sasaki (1883–1964). Yamamoto, whose popular historical novels sympathetically portray the joys and sorrows of ordinary people, has a clear, restrained style. His characters are trying to better themselves, and virtue usually triumphs. I also admire the sparse, elegant prose of Osaragi. His *Kurama Tengu* series, about a swordsman who fought for the imperial cause at the end of the Edo period (1603–1867), is my favorite. And I was a fan of Sasaki's droll humor from the time his *Classmates* was serialized in the prewar *Boys Club* magazine. I have the collected works of all three men. The death of Yojiro Ishizaka in 1986 moved me to reread his famous novels—*The Blue Mountains*, *Youth*, and *A White Bridge*.

Matsushita Electric instituted a five-day work week in 1965, some years ahead of most Japanese companies, and I tried to set either Saturday or Sunday aside for reading. Even so, there was never enough time for all the books I wanted to read. From my air conditioner division days, I left the plant at the regular quitting time and used the leisure hours to read and recharge my psychic battery. As president, I also tried to avoid staying late. My nickname was "Leaves-on-time Yamashita." Again, I see an analogy with running. Pacing yourself is crucial when you are making multimillion-dollar decisions.

Many Japanese businessmen selflessly devote themselves to their jobs. Some even take only a few days of their annual leave, and regularly stay at the office till nine or ten o'clock. I think that's unwise. As the old saying goes: "All work and no play makes Jack a dull boy." Such men know the company's problems but lose touch with everything else. Major business decisions require broad vision. Conventional wisdom says this comes as you mature, but you can only learn so much on the job. Being well read is the best way to keep informed and tap the experiences of others.

I'm an undisciplined, eclectic reader. My tastes run from natural science and astronomy to detective stories and biography. An inveterate notetaker, I always jot down new words or clever expressions and keep an encyclopedia of classical Chinese poetry by my side for handy reference. Once, many years ago, when I was trying to deal with an intractable business problem, I happened to read an anonymous poem: "Life lasts less than a hundred years, but I have a thousand years' worth of travail." The human condition hasn't changed much over the centuries. Men and women have always had to put life's vicissitudes behind them and get on with it. Learned sayings or great lines from literature make us forget, temporarily at least, our troubles.

I'm a fairly well known Go player. At age twenty, I used to think I was at least as good as a third-grade player (there are nine advanced ranks). After I became president of Matsushita Electric, the association of professional Go players, Nihon Kiin, offered me a fifth-grade rank. That was so far above my ability that I declined. Association officials assured me it was like an honorary degree, awarded in recognition of my long interest in the game, so I accepted.

Then I found that a fifth-grade Go player must play opponents of the same rank or give a handicap to lower or unranked players. I began losing regularly and the game was not so much fun any more. Fortunately, I often play with other CEOs, many of whom also seem to have received honorary rankings; I can hold my own with them.

A passion for Go transcends profession or age. My opponents have included novelist Naoki Kojima; Shoji Iwasawa, senior adviser to Mazda Motor Corp.; Hideaki Yamashita, vice president of Mitsui & Co.; Tadahiro Sekimoto, president of NEC; and Hiroshi Kojima, vice president of Sumitomo Metal Industries. I've yet to beat some of them. Another invincible foe is Kunio Ishii, a ninth-grade professional player who gives me pointers occasionally but hasn't let me win a game yet.

In 1983, the World Amateur Go Championship was held in Osaka, and Japanese and foreign players from all walks of life contended. I drew Andras Gondor, a high-school math teacher from Hungary. He used a novel strategy and beat me handily. Later I was told that the caliber of play in Europe is quite high, so I didn't feel too badly.

Occasionally I play home video games. They're fun and help to maintain hand-eye coordination, although if I become too engrossed in destroying the bad guys, my shoulders start to ache and my blood pressure goes up.

All this talk about reading and Go sounds as if I want to be completely free of Matsushita Electric, to be a full-time playboy. It did seem before I became executive advisor that I would have very little to do. I have no say in the day-to-day running of the company, of course, but a corporation is involved in many activities besides making and selling products. Matsushita's CEO, for example, cannot make courtesy calls to our plants and subsidiaries in thirty-seven countries. That is one of my duties now: to meet with and encourage employees in our far-flung operations. In 1986, I traveled to Tanzania and Peru. I don't have as much free time as I anticipated, but the assignments are worthwhile and interesting. My attitude is: "Have Matsushita philosophy, willing to travel."

Kikuko

My wife and I have a modest common agenda. We plan two mountain climbs together each year, one in Japan and one overseas. The last few years we've gone to Tateyama because the area is just right for our age and condition. The peaks are not a tough climb, but they're more than a hike in the country. Mountain climbing has brought us closer together. Photographs help us relive the journeys; we reminisce about places and people.

In the spring of 1987 we both participated in a Spartan walkathon from Osaka to Kyoto, about 25 miles. Participants were not allowed to drink or eat anything, or run during the five- to six-hour jaunt. To ward off the temptation of buying soft-drinks from roadside vending machines, before the race all contestants had to put their money into envelopes, which were officially sealed. The envelope was shown at the finish in Kyoto. Any sign of tampering resulted in automatic disqualification.

Climbing and walkathons are the main interests Kikuko and I share. Otherwise, we do our own things. About four years ago, she began studying *haiga*, a combination of painting and poetry. Devotees first paint a picture and then compose a haiku, and that is written next to the picture and complements the scene. An accomplished *haiga*-ist does both, but so far my wife only paints the picture and the teacher adds the poem. It's all beyond me. I can't tell a great combination from a double disaster. Kikuko's class holds an annual exhibition. Judging from the pictures she brings home, she is getting fairly good.

Kikuko is also learning yoga. One day at home I noticed her walking around with certain stylized movements. I thought she was practicing ballroom dancing, and commented on her new sophisticated talents. She amusedly brought me up to date on yoga.

After I became president, my wife took driving lessons and got a license. On business, I always use a company car and driver, but at other times she drives me. And on Sundays when our children bring the grandchildren for a visit, she picks them up at the nearest train station, a very short ride. One tank of gas lasts us about three months.

But to be candid, I don't enjoy riding with my wife. It's more frightening than any wind-blown mountain. As we were driving along early one morning, I saw a truck coming right at us. "This is it," I thought. My wife and the other driver both hit the brakes and the vehicles stopped inches apart. The truck driver marched over to our car, his voice dripping with contempt, and said, "You idiots. Can't you see this is one-way?" We were headed the wrong way on one of Osaka's busiest streets. Fortunately, the morning rush hour hadn't started yet.

I always sit in the back seat because it's safer. When my wife drives, the position next to the driver is the death seat as far as I'm concerned. One day I was dozing in the back and awoke just as we approached an intersection. "Step on it," I yelled. Instead she braked sharply. Looking up, I saw the signal was red. Later my wife said, "You'd better get new glasses if you're going to be a backseat driver." She won that round. Still, I think I deserve credit for riding with her.

A Division of Labor

My wife was completely in charge of raising our son and daughter. I preferred it that way and she apparently took it for granted that my role would be minimal. In our generation, the wife handled child-rearing; today, both parents are involved, especially in decisions about education.

All parents worry about how their offspring will weather the storms of puberty and adolescence. Our kids never gave us any trouble. I don't know if my wife was a supermother or the kids were naturally well behaved. Whatever the reason, I never had to worry about them.

In many Japanese families, the wife and children join forces against the father, who is busy with his career and is almost never home. Fathers often become Dagwood Bumstead–like buffoon figures or scapegoats; their children don't respect them. There are many newspaper stories and TV sit-coms about wives who hand their husband a divorce notice the day he retires. The woman only "stuck it out" while he was bringing home a regular paycheck. But I've been blessed in my marriage. Kikuko has always been a partner and helpmate.

We discussed financial arrangements when we got married and agreed upon a division of fiscal responsibilities. I gave Kikuko half my pay and she took care of routine household expenses—groceries, her own and the children's clothes. With the other half, I paid for ongoing expenditures like life insurance and major purchases—a refrigerator or a car. Pocket money for drinking with friends and entertainment came out of my half. Usually Japanese husbands hand over their entire pay and the wife doles out an allowance. But then she must manage the family budget from A to Z, and save for a rainy day. In the early years, when my salary was low, Kikuko occasionally asked for a "loan." My promotions gradually ended those sporadic entreaties.

We still have the same arrangement. A close friend once said, "Your wife was farsighted in making that fifty-fifty deal. Your salary didn't amount to much back in 1944, but she was thinking ahead to when you would be president of Matsushita." Somehow I doubt that Kikuko looked in a crystal ball then—when Japan was losing the war and U.S. air raids were imminent—and imagined that phone call from Mr. Matsushita in 1977.

Many years ago a friend, whom I shall call Tanaka, pulled a fast one on his wife. He told her Matsushita Electric was a poor company and only paid one bonus yearly. The practice then, as now, was for companies to pay summer and year-end bonuses, each equivalent to two to four months' pay, depending on business conditions. Tanaka annually pocketed several hundred dollars this way. His luck ran out when he moved to company housing near us and his wife stopped by to talk to Kikuko. By then suspicious, she said, "I understand some Matsushita employees receive two bonuses a year. My husband only gets one. Do you know how the system works?" That was the end of Tanaka's bar-hopping days. My stock rose at home as Kikuko realized what a fair and honest fellow she had married.

When I was running the air conditioner division, the wife of a subordinate complained to Kikuko, "Please tell your husband not to invite mine out drinking every night. My husband gets home very late, but he doesn't have the constitution for carousing. I'm worried about his health. Please ask Mr. Yamashita to limit the running around together to two or three nights a week." The story made me laugh: I had never gone drinking with the guy. I could imagine his line: "Gee, honey, I need some extra pocket money because Mr. Yamashita always wants to go out drinking after work. He's the boss. I can't refuse." It was a delicate situation. My junior colleague would have been furious at his wife if he knew her complaint had revealed my unwitting role as drinking buddy. One day, in an offhand way, I said to him, "Don't overdo it." He got the message.

I enjoy social drinking with co-workers and friends. Having to finance outings from my half of my salary was a good fiscal restraint. I didn't go to outrageously expensive nightclubs and hostess bars or drink too much, and I usually got home at a reasonable hour.

I expected Kikuko to be there and have a snack or a nightcap ready. During the day she was free to lunch with friends or shop—anything she wanted to do—but it was her duty to be home when I arrived. Some feminists call this male chauvinism. I saw it as Kikuko's job.

Matsushita Electric starts work at eight-thirty, and I usually was at the office by about eight. This didn't go unnoticed; I got a reputation for diligence and conscientiousness that wasn't wholly deserved. If I left the company early, everyone assumed that it was for a business meeting. Often this was the case. However, I usually declined the informal follow-up sessions, where the whiskey and banter flow till the wee hours, and went home. I got much more sleep than most people thought. That was the idea, of course.

In my thirties and forties, without seven hours' sleep, I felt sluggish the next day. Now, five or six hours are enough, which seems to be a little less than my contemporaries need. On the other hand, I often doze in the car when I'm being driven somewhere on company business. I can sleep anywhere.

I don't have strong likes and dislikes in food, but I must watch my weight carefully. Kikuko fixes me a special salad for breakfast with about ten different vegetables. She boils winter squash, potatoes, and carrots. After they cool, she adds lettuce, cucumber, tomato, radish, and other items depending on the season, and tosses them with a dressing. Delicious and inexpensive! It's usually all I eat in the morning.

I don't do any housework. I've never washed or dried a dish, or gone shopping with Kikuko. Fortunately, my wife has rarely been sick. When our daughter was living at home, she helped out. If a man has to work all day and take care of the house, too, what's the point of having a wife? If that sounds old-fashioned, so be it.

I don't want to leave the impression that I'm one of those helpless Japanese husbands who can't get dressed in the morning without his wife's help. I can do whatever I have to. I always did my own laundry on overseas trips and my shirts looked pretty good, if I say so myself. That way I didn't need to take along many clothes. Some Matsushita men posted away from Osaka on temporary assignment have their wives send them clean shirts and underwear every three weeks! By comparison, I was quite self-sufficient.

I have much to be thankful for, especially good health. It was a rare privilege to work with Konosuke Matsushita and my colleagues at Matsushita Electric, and to lead the company for nine years.

I've never considered myself brilliant or profound. So I have no dramatic message, no sure-fire success formula to impart to aspiring executives. I wrote this book in the hope that readers would say, "If Yamashita could do it, so can I." I think that's the lesson of my career.